THE COMPLETE BOOK OF DEFENSIVE FOOTBALL DRILLS

Jerry Tolley

Former Head Football Coach
Elon University

ISBN: 1-58518-911-1
Library of Congress Control Number: 2004112088
Book layout and diagrams: Deborah Oldenburg
Cover design: Jeanne Hamilton
Front cover photo: Jonathan Daniel/Getty Images

Coaches Choice
P.O. Box 1828
Monterey, CA 93942
www.coacheschoice.com

Dedication

It is with great pride that I dedicate this book to the players, coaches, managers, trainers, and administrators who played for and/or supported the Elon College (now Elon University) football team during my tenure as head football coach from 1977–1981. Because of their dedication, Elon was able to capture four conference titles, play in three national championship games, and win back-to-back national titles in 1980 and 1981.

I would like to pay a special tribute to my valuable assistant coaches, Mickey Brown, Macky Carden, Linwood Ferguson, Clayton Johnson, and Don Kelly. Without their hard work, dedication, and knowledge of football, we would not have achieved such success. I was honored to have them as members of my coaching staff.

Also, I would like to extend whole-hearted thanks and sincere appreciation to the special young men who were members of the football team. These dedicated football players gave their all and through their determination and hard work, led the team to an unprecedented era of football excellence. Their five-year record of 49-11-2 is unparalleled in both the state of North Carolina and in the annals of Elon's rich football history. On the Elon campus, their unprecedented accomplishments on the gridiron will always be remembered as the Golden Era of Elon football.

In particular, I would like to pay special tribute to my football captains, Roxie Bratton, Donavan Brown,* Bryan Burney, Bill Devaney, Bobby Hedrick, Wes McLaughlin, Randy Reid, Johnny Richards, Keith Richardson, Jimmy Riddle,* Adrian Robertson, Ernie Tootoo, and Chris Worst.* These were the players who led the team both on and off the field. Never has a head coach been so blessed with such an outstanding group of young athletes and leaders. They were not only exceptional football players but also served as coaches on the field and role models for the entire Elon athletic family.

And finally, I would like to single out Dr. Fred Young, president of Elon College (1973–1998), Dr. Alan White, Elon's athletics director, and Mr. Melvin Shreves, assistant athletics director. They not only provided the football program with the needed financial support, but were also the team's most loyal fans. You could always count on them to be at every game, cheering the team to victory.

* *Two-year captains*

Acknowledgments

Sincere appreciation is expressed to the many outstanding coaches who have contributed defensive drills to this book. Their commitment to the time-honored tradition of sharing ideas among the coaching fraternity made the editorship of this publication both an honor and a privilege.*

Gratitude is expressed to Kristin Simonetti, a student at Elon University, for her editorial assistance and masterful job of typing the manuscript. Also thanked is Pat Whelan for her administrative support. Mr. Kyle Wills, a friend and associate athletics director at Elon, is acknowledged for the illustrations accompanying each drill.

A loving appreciation is expressed to my wonderful wife, Joanie, for her patience, understanding, and support.

*Special appreciation is extended to each of the contributing coaches who verified that all compiled biographical information was accurate. It should be noted that all biographical information was current as of September 1, 2003.

Contents

Foreword

It is indeed a privilege to introduce Jerry Tolley's new comprehensive book of defensive football drills. A National Coach of the Year, Dr. Tolley is a former Elon University football coach who won back-to-back National Championships in 1980 and 1981. His overall winning percentage of 80.6 is believed to be among the highest in collegiate circles. His three-year national playoff bowl record of 8 wins and 1 loss is most impressive.

His latest publication, *The Complete Book of Defensive Football Drills*, contains drills fundamental to every defensive position, as well as drills to teach and practice tackling, team pursuit. and general agility. Also included are drills to develop and maintain a desired level of cardiovascular endurance.

Specific safety factors are highlighted with each drill and should prove to be an invaluable source of knowledge for the seasoned veteran as well as the neophyte. Detailed medical and legal considerations, as well as comprehensive guidelines for conducting two-a-day pre-season practices, are included in the appendices.

This extraordinary drill book has application for every football coach from the Pop Warner League to the professional ranks, and I enthusiastically introduce it to the coaching profession. It should prove to be a most useful addition to every coach's professional library.

– William "Mack" Brown
Head Football Coach
The University Of Texas at Austin

Defensive Line Drills

CLOSE THE CUSHION

Mike Bellotti
University of California-Davis, California State University-Hayward,
Weber State University, California State University-Chico, University of Oregon

Objective: To teach and practice the proper fundamentals and techniques of rushing the passer. Special emphasis is placed on reacting to and exploding off the snap of the ball and closing the distance (cushion) between the pass blocker and the pass rusher as quickly as possible.

Equipment Needed: Football and cone

Description:

- Position an offensive lineman in a two-point stance, with his outside foot back, two yards off a selected line of scrimmage.
- Align a defensive lineman in an outside *shade* position to the offensive lineman.
- The coach is positioned over the football at the center position.
- A cone is placed 10 yards behind the coach (see diagram).
- Other drill participants stand adjacent to the drill area and alternate as pass rushers and pass blockers.
- On the coach's cadence and ball snap, the offensive lineman backpedals in a straight line and as fast as possible past the cone.
- The defensive lineman reacts to the center snap and explodes upfield in an attempt to close the *cushion* by tagging the blocker on his outside shoulder with his outside arm.
- After touching the offensive lineman, the pass rusher finishes the drill by sprinting past the cone.
- The drill continues until all drill participants have had a sufficient number of repetitions from both the left and right.
- The drill can be run with paired defensive and offensive linemen executing the drill at the same time.

Coaching Points:

- Always check to see that defensive linemen are in their three-point stance and are crowding the football as much as possible (they are playing pass all the way).
- As the defensive linemen *explode* out of their stance, emphasize the importance of having the back foot replace the down hand as they move forward.
- Instruct the defensive linemen to reach with their outside arm when they touch the upfield shoulder of the offensive linemen.
- Insist that the defensive linemen finish the drill by sprinting past the cone.

Safety Considerations:

- A proper warm-up should precede the drill.
- The drill area should be clear of all foreign articles.
- The drill should progress from form work to full speed.
- When executing the drill with two offensive and defensive linemen, a minimum of seven yards should separate the paired drill participants.

Variations:

- Can vary the pre-aligned depth of the offensive linemen as well as the depth of the cone.
- Can be used as a *competition* drill by choosing sides and keeping count of the number of successful touches.
- Can position a manager (quarterback) at the cone position and have pass rushers strip the football.

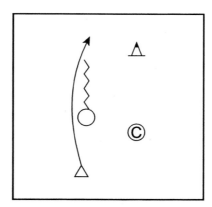

BIG BAGS

Pete Carroll
University of Arkansas, Iowa State University, North Carolina State University,
University of the Pacific, Buffalo Bills, Minnesota Vikings, San Francisco 49ers,
New York Jets, New England Patriots, University of Southern California
National Champions: Southern California 2003
National Coach of the Year: Southern California 2003

Objective: To teach and practice the proper fundamentals of rushing the passer. Skills related to tackling and stripping the football from the quarterback's hand are also incorporated.

Equipment Needed: Four pop-up dummies, one tackling dummy, two footballs (one painted green)

Description:

- Place four pop-up dummies in a straight line and perpendicular to a selected line of scrimmage. Five yards should separate each of the pop-up dummies. A tackling dummy is placed five yards behind and at a 45-degree angle from the fourth pop-up dummy. A football is placed on top of the tackling dummy (see diagram).

- Position a defensive lineman in a three-point sprinter's stance and in the designated technique alignment to the row of dummies.

- Other defensive linemen stand adjacent to the drill area.

- The coach (center) is positioned over a green football three yards in front of the pop-up dummies and in the proper center relationship to the pass rushing defensive lineman. (The football is painted green so it will be the same color as the grass, forcing the defensive lineman to really focus on the football as it is snapped.)

- On the coach's cadence and ball snap, the defensive lineman drives out of his stance and executes alternating right and left *club/rip* techniques on the four pop-up dummies.

- After contacting the fourth pop-up dummy, the defensive lineman sprints to, and executes a right shoulder tackle on, the tackling dummy while stripping the football with the left hand.

- The drill continues until all defensive linemen have had a sufficient number of repetitions.

- The drill should be conducted from both a left and right tackling dummy alignment.

Coaching Points:

- Always check to see that defensive linemen are aligned correctly and are in their proper pass-rush stances.
- Emphasize the importance of crowding the tip of the football and *getting off* on the snap of the football as quickly as possible with hands high and tight.
- Make sure all defensive linemen use the proper technique in executing the *club/rip*.
- Insist that the drill be conducted at full speed.
- Make sure the defensive linemen practice the proper fundamentals and techniques of stripping the football and safe tackling.

Safety Considerations:

- A proper warm-up should precede the drill.
- The drill should progress from form work to full speed.
- Full equipment should be worn.
- The drill area should be clear of all foreign articles.
- Instruct all defensive ends in the proper fundamentals and techniques of stripping the football and executing a safe tackle.

Variations:

- Can be used with defensive linemen executing a *club/over* technique.

- Can be used with a tighter alignment of the pop-up dummies (six inches apart) (this alignment will improve the defensive linemen's reaction time).

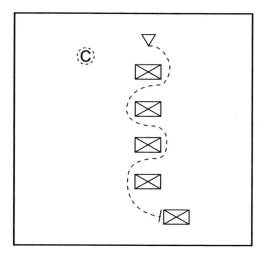

SHED TACKLING

David N. Cutcliffe
University of Tennessee, University of Mississippi
National Assistant Coach of the Year: Tennessee 1998

Objective: To teach and practice the proper fundamentals and techniques of defeating reach and veer blocks. The skills of gaining separation from the blocker and locating and executing a tackle on a ballcarrier are also incoporated.

Equipment Needed: Footballs

Description:

- Position an offensive lineman on a selected line of scrimmage. A ballcarrier is aligned in a *shade* position five yards behind the offensive lineman.
- Align a defensive lineman in an outside *shade* position over the offensive lineman (see diagrams).
- The coach is positioned over the football at the center position.
- Other drill participants stand adjacent to the drill area.
- On the coach's cadence and ball snap, the offensive lineman executes the assigned block (reach or veer) and the ballcarrier runs the designated running path.
- The defensive lineman reacts to, and defeats the block of, the offensive lineman and executes a *form* tackle on the ballcarrier.
- The drill continues until all defensive linemen have had a sufficient number of repetitions.
- The drill should be conducted both left and right.

Coaching Points:

- Always check to see that defensive linemen are aligned correctly and are in their proper stances.
- Instruct the defensive linemen to *fire* their feet and to maintain a squared pad relationship to the line of scrimmage while attacking the blocker.
- When reacting to and defeating the reach block, instruct the defensive linemen to gain separation with the hands and locate and tackle the ballcarrier (see diagram A).
- Instruct the defensive linemen to attack the blocker with extended arms to prevent him from blocking the linebacker when reacting to and defeating the veer block. The defensive linemen then execute a *form* tackle on the ballcarrier, who is cutting back (see diagram B).

- In executing the *form* tackle, instruct the defensive linemen to focus their eyes on the far armpit of the ballcarrier and make contact by wrapping the arm, *grabbing cloth*, and running the feet through the *form* tackle.
- Make sure all defensive linemen practice the proper fundamentals and techniques of safe tackling.

Safety Considerations:

- A proper warm-up should precede the drill.
- The drill area should be clear of all foreign articles.
- The drill should progress from form work to full speed (never live tackling).
- The coach should closely monitor the intensity of the drill, especially the *tempo* of the ballcarriers.
- Instruct all defensive linemen in the proper fundamentals and techniques of safe tackling.

Variations:

- Can be used with the ballcarriers holding a hand shield.
- Can use the pad of a sled instead of an offensive lineman to react to and defeat the reach block.

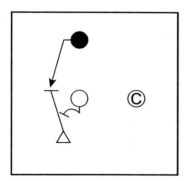 

CONTAIN DRILL*

Bill McCartney
University of Colorado
National Champions: 1990
National Coach of the Year: 1989

Objective: To teach and practice interior pursuit with special emphasis on reacting to the ball snap and taking the proper angle to the ballcarrier.

Equipment Needed: 20 cones and four footballs

Description:

- Align ten cones, one each, on every five-yard line downfield from a selected line of scrimmage. All cones are placed five yards from each sideline (see diagram).

- A center and a quarterback are positioned over a football at midfield.

- A runner, holding a football, is positioned between cones and sidelines. A manager or another player is placed behind each runner.

- Align the defensive front in a huddle behind the line of scrimmage.

- Alternating defensive fronts stand adjacent to the drill area.

- On the coach's command, the defensive front breaks the huddle with an assigned defensive call and takes their positions over the football.

- On the cadence and ball snap, the quarterback takes a five-yard pass drop and passes the football to the manager on either sideline. When the manager catches the football, the ballcarrier on that sideline sprints downfield.

- The defensive linemen react to the ball snap and carry out the initial steps of the designated defense called in the huddle. They then take their proper pursuit angle to the ballcarrier.

- When the pursuers get to the ballcarrier, they break down and wait for the coach's whistle to end the drill.

- The drill continues with alternating defensive fronts pursuing both left and right from midfield and both hash marks.

* Reprinted with permission from *101 Winning Football Drills: From the Legends of the Game* by Jerry Tolley

Coaching Points:

• Always check to see that all personnel are aligned correctly and are in their proper stances.

• The drill should progress from walk-through to full speed.

• Make sure the defenders execute the initial steps of the assigned defense before going in pursuit.

Safety Considerations:

• A proper warm-up should precede the drill.

• The drill area should be clear of all foreign articles. This includes the sideline areas.

Variations:

• Can be used by the entire defensive team.

• Can align ballcarriers at various positions on the sideline or at other positions on the field.

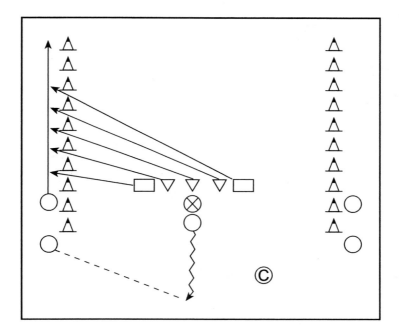

BLOCK SHEDDING AND AVOIDANCE DRILL

Harvey Hyde
University of Hawaii, Pasadena City College, University of Nevada at Las Vegas
National Champions: Pasadena City College 1977, 1978, and 1983

Objective: To teach and practice the proper fundamentals and techniques of executing a forearm-shoulder blow.

Equipment Needed: One-man blocking sled

Description:

- Position defensive linemen in a straight line in front of a one-man blocking sled. The first lineman is positioned one yard in front of the pad and in a three-point stance.
- On the coach's command, the first defensive lineman explodes out of his stance and strikes a forearm-shoulder blow to the sled.
- On the coach's second command, the lineman separates from the sled using various release techniques.
- The drill continues until all drill participants have had a sufficient number of left and right forearm-shoulder blows.

Coaching Points:

- Always check to see that linemen are in their proper stances.
- Make sure the desired body position is maintained throughout the drill.
- Insist that all linemen execute their blocks on the rise.
- Emphasize the importance of proper footwork.

Safety Considerations:

- A proper warm-up should precede the drill.
- Helmets should be worn with chinstraps snapped.
- Instruct linemen in the proper techniques of hitting a sled.
- The sled should be checked periodically for possible maintenance and repairs.

Variations:

- Can be used with linemen in four-point or six-point stances.
- Can have linemen execute various reactions after separating from the sled, such as pursuit and tackle, fumble recovery, and rushing a passer.

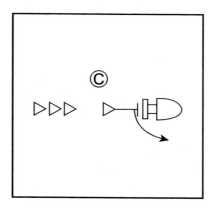

PASS RUSH

Larry R. Donovan
University of Nebraska, University of South Dakota, Washington State University,
University of Iowa, University of Kansas, University of Montana,
British Columbia Lions, Saskatchewan Roughriders, Renesas Hurricanes

Objective: To teach and practice the proper fundamentals and techniques of rushing the passer.

Equipment Needed: None

Description:

- Position defensive linemen on the hash marks of selected yard lines. All defensive linemen face the near sideline.
- A blocker is positioned in a front-facing alignment to each defensive lineman. One yard separates the blocker and defensive linemen.
- All drill participants are in the *football position*.
- On the coach's command, the first blocker assumes a pass-block stance as the defensive lineman rushes an imaginary quarterback down the yard line.
- As the defensive lineman rushes, he reaches out and *grasps* the shoulders of the blocker, locks his elbows, and leans forward.
- The blocker is instructed to retreat down the line.
- The defensive lineman now begins to push with one arm and pull with the other. As the left arm pulls, the right pushes and the right leg drives to the blocker's right foot. When the right foot comes down, the right arm pulls and the left arm pushes as the left leg drives to the blocker's left foot.
- The drill ends when the coach blows his whistle.
- The drill continues until all defensive linemen have had a sufficient number of repetitions.

Coaching Points:

- This drill should be used basically as a walk-through drill.
- Make sure the defensive linemen maintain a forward body lean throughout the drill.
- Special emphasis should be placed on the arm and leg movements. All movements are down the line and not lateral.
- Instruct the defensive linemen to keep their eyes on the imaginary passer.
- When drill is executed properly, the defensive linemen will look as if they are skating on ice.

Safety Considerations:

- A proper warm-up should precede the drill.
- Helmets should be worn with chinstraps snapped.

Variation:

- Can be used with defensive linemen coming out of a stance.

INTERIOR LINE REACTION DRILL

> **Gerry Faust**
> University of Notre Dame, University of Akron

Objective: To teach and practice the proper fundamentals and techniques used against various individual blocking schemes.

Equipment Needed: Flashcards and footballs

Description:

- Align an offensive line, including a tight end, over the football on a selected line of scrimmage. A quarterback (coach), with six flashcards, is positioned over the center.
- The defensive linemen take their regular positions over the offense (see diagram).
- Other defensive linemen stand adjacent to drill area.
- The defensive line coach stands behind the defense.
- On the coach's cadence and ball snap, each of the offensive linemen executes one of six designated blocks as shown on the flashcards.
- The defensive linemen read and react to the individual blocks.
- After each play, the offense returns to the huddle to review the flashcards as the defensive coach makes comments and corrections.
- The drill continues until alternating defensive fronts have had a sufficient number of repetitions.

Coaching Points:

- Always check to see that defensive linemen are aligned correctly and are in their proper stances.
- The six flashcards should show only opponent's blocks at various offensive positions and not their blocking schemes for various plays.
- The defensive line coach should make only coaching comments and corrections while the offense is in the huddle.
- Emphasize the importance of executing as many repetitions as possible.

Safety Considerations:

- A proper warm-up should precede the drill.
- The drill should progress from walk-through to full speed (full speed to contact only).
- The coach should closely monitor the intensity of the drill.
- Flashcards must be drawn up so one player's reaction will not take him into an adjacent player.

Variation:

- Can be used as a form or live drill.

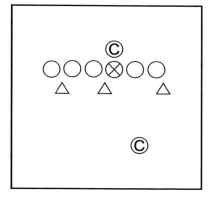

LADDER CLIMB-PURSUIT

Jimmy Wyne Feix
Western Kentucky University

Objective: To teach and practice the proper fundamentals and techniques of rushing the passer and pursuing to the football after the pass is thrown. Skills related to agility, reaction, and quickness are also incorporated.

Equipment Needed: Footballs

Description:

- Align a quarterback (coach), holding a football, at the midpoint of a selected line of scrimmage.
- Position the defensive linemen in their regular alignments across the line of scrimmage.
- Place three receivers on a yard line 10 yards downfield. With 10 yards separating each of the three receivers (see diagram).
- Other defensive linemen stand adjacent to the drill area.
- On cadence and snap count, the quarterback (coach) executes various pass drops. The defensive linemen drive out of their stances and initiate their pass rushes.
- When the coach sets to pass, all defensive linemen jump vertically as high as possible with their arms up (*ladder climb*).
- As linemen jump, the passer scrambles either left or right and again sets to pass. The defensive linemen redirect their charge and again execute their vertical jumps. This procedure is repeated a third time.
- The quarterback then passes the football to one of the three receivers downfield. The three pass rushers sprint to the football and assume a *break down* position working their feet. The drill is completed when the coach blows his whistle.
- The drill continues until rotating defensive fronts have had a sufficient number of repetitions from various field positions.

Coaching Points:

- Always check to see that defensive linemen are aligned correctly and are in their proper stances.
- Instruct defensive linemen to stay in their proper lanes as they rush the passer.
- In executing the *ladder climb*, insist that the defensive linemen jump straight up.
- Make sure defensive linemen sprint to the football after the pass is thrown.

Safety Considerations:

- A proper warm-up should precede the drill.
- Drill area should be clear of all foreign articles.
- Instruct defensive linemen to break down two yards in front of the receivers and to avoid all contact with them.

Variations:

- Can be used with any number of defensive linemen.
- Can incorporate defensive ends.
- Can place dummies directly across from line of scrimmage for pass rushers to step over.

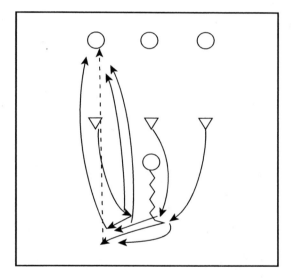

DEFEATING THE BLOCK*

William D. "Bill" Murray (Deceased)
[Drill submitted by Dr. Michael "Mike" McGee]
University of Delaware, Duke University
College Football Hall of Fame: 1974
Amos Alonzo Stagg Award: 1971
AFCA President: 1963
AFCA Executive Director: 1966-1981

Objective: To teach and practice proper fundamentals and techniques of defeating the drive block. The drill stresses the importance of achieving a shoe-to-shoe relationship to the opponent before defeating his block. It also stresses the necessity of maintaining a parallel (squared) shoulder and hip relationship to the line of scrimmage until the direction of the ballcarrier is determined. The drill is conducted in two stages.

Equipment Needed: Footballs

Description:

Stage I–Ballcarrier's Path is Determined

- Align a blocker and ballcarrier in their proper relationship to a selected line of scrimmage.
- A defensive lineman is placed in one of three positions: behind the blocker, head-up the blocker, and ahead of the blocker (see diagrams A, B, and C).
- On the coach's cadence, the defender reacts to and defeats the block of the offensive lineman and then executes the tackle on the ballcarrier.
- The drill continues until all participants have had a sufficient number of repetitions.
- The drill should be executed both left and right.

Stage II–Ballcarrier's Path is Undetermined

- Personnel are align in the same relative position as in Stage I, descriptions 1 and 2.
- In Stage II, the path of the runner is undetermined and the runner can cut off the offensive lineman's block either left or right (see diagrams D, E, and F).
- On the coach's cadence, the defensive lineman reacts to and defeats the block of the offensive lineman and executes the tackle on the ballcarrier.
- The drill continues until all the linemen have had a sufficient number of repetitions.
- The drill should be run both left and right.

* Reprinted with permission from *101 Winning Football Drills: From the Legends of the Game* by Jerry Tolley

Coaching Points:

- Always check to see that the defensive linemen are aligned correctly and are in their proper stances.
- It is imperative that the defenders achieve a shoe-to-shoe relationship with the blocker before extension.
- The defenders should use only the amount of force necessary to defeat the blocks and then gain separation for the tackle.
- Instruct the defensive linemen to maintain a squared-shoulder and hip relationship to the ballcarrier until the ballcarrier's running path has been determined.
- Make sure the defenders use the proper fundamentals and techniques in executing the tackle.

Safety Considerations:

- It is imperative that a proper warm-up precede this drill.
- Instruct all the defenders in the proper fundamentals and techniques of defeating a block and executing a safe tackle.
- The drill should progress from formwork to live work.
- The coach should watch for and eliminate all unacceptable matchups as to size and athletic ability.
- The coach should monitor closely the intensity of the drill.

Variations:

- Can be used as a form or live drill.
- Can be used as an offensive line drill.

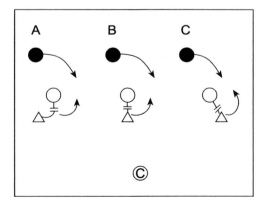
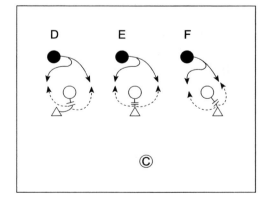

LOCK OUT AND SHUFFLE

Steve R. Furness (Deceased)
Michigan State University, Indianapolis Colts, Pittsburgh Steelers

Objective: To teach and practice the proper fundamentals and techniques of using the hands in defeating a block. Skills related to reaction and agility are also incorporated.

Equipment Needed: None

Description:

- Align a row of designated offensive linemen five yards apart in front of a selected line of scrimmage.
- Position a defensive lineman in a front-facing alignment to each blocker.
- The coach stands behind the defense.
- On the coach's command, the first offensive lineman drives from his stance and executes a left shoulder drive block against the front-facing defensive lineman.
- The defensive lineman reacts to the charge of the blocker by *shuffling* to his right and driving both his hands to his opponent's numbers. (His hands should work from the numbers to the shoulder area.)
- The drill continues until all defensive linemen have had a sufficient number of repetitions.
- The drill should be conducted both left and right.
- Blockers and defensive linemen can be interchanged at the discretion of the coach.

Coaching Points:

- Always check to see that defensive linemen are in their proper stances.
- Instruct the defensive linemen to approach the line of scrimmage as the blockers initiate their blocks.
- It is imperative that the defensive linemen lock out their arms as they contact the blockers and shuffle either left or right.

Safety Considerations:

- A proper warm-up should precede the drill.
- The drill area should be clear of all foreign articles.
- Maintain a minimum distance of five yards between each pair of drill participants.
- The coach should look for and eliminate all unacceptable match-ups of size and athletic ability.
- The drill should progress from walk-through to full speed (not live).
- The coach should closely monitor the intensity of the drill.
- Paired drill participants are instructed to execute the drill one at a time.

Variations:

- Can be used with defensive linemen executing other block-defeating techniques.
- Can be used as a defensive end or linebacker drill.

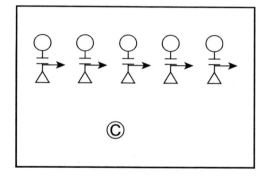

PASS RUSH DRILL

Paul D. Wiggin
San Francisco 49ers, Kansas City Chiefs, New Orleans Saints,
Stanford University, Minnesota Vikings

Objective: To teach and practice the proper fundamentals and techniques of defeating the pass block and maintaining the proper lane relationship in rushing the passer.

Equipment Needed: None

Description:

- Chalk in a pass rush diagram on a selected line of scrimmage (see diagram).
- Position an offensive lineman in his normal alignment on the selected line of scrimmage.
- Place a quarterback in a pass drop position 7.5 yards behind the line of scrimmage.
- A defensive lineman is positioned over the offensive blocker (see diagram).
- Other defensive and offensive linemen stand adjacent to the drill area.
- On the coach's cadence and snap count, one defensive lineman at a time rushes the passer using various pass rushing techniques to get past the pass blocker. He is instructed to maintain his proper lane relationship to the quarterback (see diagram).
- The drill continues until all defensive linemen have had a sufficient number of repetitions. A minimum of three repetitions is recommended.

Safety Considerations:

- It is imperative that a proper warm-up precede the drill.
- The drill area should be clear of all foreign articles.
- The coach should watch for and eliminate all unacceptable match-ups of size and athletic ability.
- The drill should progress from form work to live work.
- The coach should closely monitor the intensity of the drill.
- Only one pair of drill participants should execute the drill at a time.
- Instruct the blockers never to cut block the pass rushers.

Variation:

• Can be used as an offensive line pass protection drill.

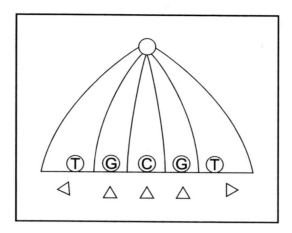

POWER PASS RUSH DRILL

Dean O. Slayton
University Texas at El Paso, Howard Payne University,
University of North Texas, Texas Tech University

Objective: To teach and practice the proper techniques and fundamentals in the execution of the *power rush* when rushing the passer.

Equipment Needed: Blocking chute (five stalls 48" high and 48" wide), four hand shields, and football

Description:

- Align defensive linemen in waves behind the four stalls of the blocking chute.
- Position a pass blocker holding a hand shield in front of each stall.
- The coach, with a football, is positioned in the middle chute.
- On the coach's command, the first wave of defensive linemen takes their stances under the chute. On the coach's cadence and ball snap, the defensive linemen fire out of their stances and drive the shield holders back five yards.
- The defensive linemen then execute an escape technique such as the *swim* and then sprint five yards up-field to complete the drill.
- The drill continues until all defensive linemen have had a sufficient number of repetitions.

Coaching Points:

- Always check to see that defensive linemen are aligned correctly and are in their proper stances.
- Shield holders should be instructed to strenuously resist the rush of the defensive linemen.
- Insist that defensive linemen stay in their proper pass rushing lanes.
- Make sure the defensive linemen maintain the desired body position throughout the drill.

Safety Considerations:

- A proper warm-up should precede the drill.
- The coach should watch for and eliminate all unacceptable match-ups of size and athletic ability.
- The drill should progress from form work to full speed.
- The coach should closely monitor the intensity of the drill.

Variation:

- Can incorporate a quarterback for pass rushers to redirect on after they execute their escape technique.

INTERIOR LINE PURSUIT DRILL

Hornsby Howell
North Carolina A&T State University, University of Georgia, Shaw University

Objective: To teach and practice interior pursuit with special emphasis placed on taking the proper pursuit angles.

Equipment Needed: Footballs

Description:

- Align a quarterback (coach) and offensive front over the football at the midpoint of a selected line of scrimmage.
- Position a defensive interior front over the offense (see diagram).
- Place a receiver on the line of scrimmage on each sideline.
- Other drill participants stand adjacent to the drill area.
- On the coach's cadence and ball snap, the defensive linemen react to and defeat the drive blocks of the offensive linemen.
- The quarterback (coach) then passes the football to one of the receivers on the sideline.
- The defensive linemen redirect their initial charge and pursue the receiver, who is sprinting down the sideline.
- The drill continues until all defensive linemen have had a sufficient number of repetitions from midfield and both hash marks.

Coaching Points:

- Always check to see that the defensive linemen are aligned correctly and are in their proper stances.
- Make sure that all defensive linemen react to the block of the offensive linemen before they take their instructed pursuit angle.
- Insist that the defensive linemen pursue the receiver at full speed.

Safety Considerations:

- A proper warm-up should precede the drill.
- Drill area should be clear of all foreign articles. This includes the sideline areas.
- Instruct all personnel that there should be minimum contact at the line of scrimmage.

Variations:

- Can incorporate other defensive personnel.
- Can be used as a conditioning drill.

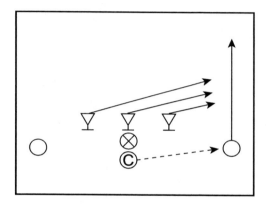

PURSUIT, SHED TACKLE, AND FUMBLE RECOVERY DRILL

Don D. Turner
Imperial Valley Junior College, Santa Barbara City College,
University of California-Santa Barbara, University Minnesota-Morris,
United States International University, Bemidji State University,
Eastern Oregon University, Chadron State College, University of Dubuque,
Bethany College (WV), Birmingham (England) Bulls

Objective: To teach and practice the proper fundamentals and techniques of defeating a blocker, pursuing a ballcarrier, and executing a tackle. Incorporated are skills related to recovering a fumble.

Equipment Needed: Five large blocking dummies and footballs

Description:

- Lay four large blocking dummies in a row three yards apart and perpendicular to a selected line of scrimmage. Stand another blocking dummy five yards down from, and adjacent to, the back plane of the other dummies (see diagram). A football is placed on top of the standup dummy.

- Position a row of defensive linemen one yard to the outside and one yard back of the dummy area. A row of blockers is aligned in a corresponding position to the dummies and facing the defensive linemen.

- On the coach's command, the first two drill participants move in and out of the space between the dummies. The blockers are instructed to execute high shoulder blocks. The defensive linemen counter with near-arm-near-leg *rip* techniques to the outside shoulders of the blockers as they make contact between dummies.

- After the defensive lineman sheds the final block, he executes a left shoulder tackle on the standup dummy.

- As the football on top of the dummy flies free, the tackler scrambles for the fumble recovery.

- The drill continues until all defensive linemen have had a sufficient number of repetitions.

- The drill should be conducted both left and right. When the drill is conducted to the right, a right shoulder tackle is executed.

Coaching Points:

- Instruct the defensive linemen to *shuffle* down the line and not to use cross-over steps.
- Make sure defensive linemen maintain a good *football position* with their shoulders square to the line of scrimmage throughout the drill.
- It is imperative that the defensive linemen keep the outside arm free.
- Make sure defensive linemen practice the proper fundamentals and techniques of safe tackling.

Safety Considerations:

- A proper warm-up should precede the drill.
- Instruct blockers to use only high shoulder blocks.
- The coach should watch for and eliminate all unacceptable match-ups of size and athletic ability.
- The drill should progress from form work to full speed.
- The coach should closely monitor the intensity of the drill.
- Instruct all personnel in the proper fundamentals of safe tackling and fumble recovering.

Variations:

- Can be used as a form or live drill.
- Can be executed with the defensive lineman shuffling over and through the dummies.
- Can incorporate a ballcarrier in the place of the standup dummy.
- Can be used as a linebacker and defensive end drill.

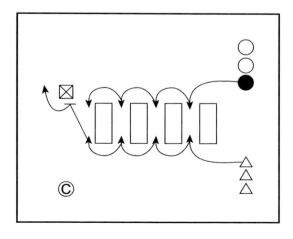

TWO-MAN SLED HIT PROGRESSION*

Leonard J. "Len" Casanova (Deceased)
Santa Clara University, University of Pittsburgh, University of Oregon
College Football Hall of Fame: 1977
Amos Alonzo Stagg Award: 1990
AFCA President: 1964

Objective: To teach and practice the proper fundamentals and techniques in the execution of the forearm-shoulder blow.

Equipment Needed: Two-man sled

Description:

- Position two rows of defensive linemen behind the pads of a two-man sled. The drill is conducted in six phases as follows:
    - *Forearm Lift.* The first two linemen assume the football position in front of the pads of the sled and, on the coach's command, strike the pad using only the inside fist and forearm.
    - *Hip Thrust.* The paired drill participants assume knee stances sitting back on their heels. On the coach's command, they lean forward at a 45-degree angle and strike a forearm blow to the pads. In the execution of the blow, the head is up, the outside arm is thrown forward, and the hips are extended thrusting the belt buckle toward the pad.
    - *Step and Hit.* In this phase, the defensive linemen assume their normal stances and, on the coach's command, step with the inside foot as they strike the pad with a forearm blow. The outside foot does not move.
    - *Hit and Gather.* Repeat procedures in the preceding phase bringing the outside foot to a good football position on the sled. Hold for four seconds.
    - *Hit, Gather, and Move Feet.* Repeat the preceding two phases working both feet in place without moving the sled.
    - *Drive.* Repeat the preceding three phases with linemen driving the sled until the coach blows his whistle. The drill participants now execute a seat roll to complete drill.
- The drill continues until all the defensive linemen have had a sufficient number of repetitions of all six drill phases.
- The drill should be conducted with the linemen executing both left and right forearm-shoulder blows.

* Reprinted with permission from *101 Winning Football Drills: From the Legends of the Game* by Jerry Tolley

Coaching Points:

- Always check to see that the linemen are in their proper stances in the last four phases (*Step and Hit* through *Drive*).
- Instruct the linemen to keep their shoulders square to the pad of the sled throughout all phases of the drill.
- In contacting the pad, make sure the arm is bent to form a 90-degree blocking-angle surface with the wrist rotated inward.
- Insist that the linemen maintain a good hitting position with the head up and feet apart throughout this drill.
- The coach should always view the drill from behind the drill participants.

Safety Considerations:

- A proper warm-up should precede the drill.
- Helmets should be worn with chinstraps snapped.
- Instruct all the linemen in the proper fundamentals and techniques of blocking a sled.
- The sled should be checked periodically for possible maintenance and repairs.

Variation:

- Can be used as a defensive end and linebacker drill.

RECOIL

Lyle R. Setencich
Boise State University, California Poly State University, University of the Pacific, Arizona State University, University of California, Texas Tech University

Objective: To teach and practice the proper fundamentals and techniques of shedding a blocker, pursuing a ballcarrier, and executing a tackle.

Equipment Needed: Footballs

Description:

- Align two rows of linemen in front-facing positions adjacent to the sideline and across a selected line of scrimmage (see diagram). Designate one row as blockers and the other row as tacklers. One yard separates the blockers and tacklers.

- A ballcarrier is positioned five yards behind the first blocker.

- On the coach's command, the first two drill participants break down in a *football position*. After holding for two counts, the blocker *bellies back* and then up as the tackler shuffles down the line.

- As the blocker *bellies back* to the line of scrimmage, he executes an upper-body shoulder block and the tacklers counter with a two-hand hand shiver. This procedure is repeated two additional times.

- After executing the third two-hand hand *shiver*, the defender executes a form tackle on the ballcarrier who has been running five yards behind and parallel to the blocker.

- The drill continues until all drill participants have executed a sufficient number of repetitions.

- The drill should be conducted both left and right and between the sideline and hash marks.

- Blockers and tacklers can be interchanged at the discretion of the coach.

Coaching Points:

- Instruct the defensive linemen to maintain a good *football position* with their shoulders parallel to the line of scrimmage as they execute the shuffle.

- In the execution of the two-hand hand *shiver*, make sure the defenders' thumbs are up and their elbows are down.

- Make sure that defensive linemen practice the proper fundamentals of safe tackling.

Safety Considerations:

- A proper warm-up should precede the drill.
- The drill area should be clear of all foreign articles. This includes the sideline areas.
- Instruct blockers to execute only high blocks.
- The drill should progress from form work to live work.
- The coach should closely monitor the intensity of the drill.
- Instruct all defensive linemen in the proper fundamentals and techniques of safe tackling.

Variations:

- Can be used as a form or live drill.
- Can be used without the ballcarrier.
- Can be used with a varying number of blocker–defensive lineman contacts before the form tackle is executed.

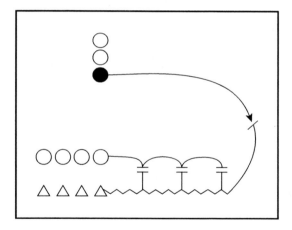

SHED DRILL

John W. Anderson (Deceased)
Dartmouth College, Cornell University, Middlebury College, Brown University

Objective: To teach and practice the proper fundamentals and techniques of shedding a block.

Equipment Needed: None

Description:

- Position two rows of defensive linemen adjacent to each other and across a selected line of scrimmage (see diagram). Three yards should separate all drill participants.
- On the coach's command, the first lineman in each row executes a left *shoulder rip* technique.
- The description is repeated with each lineman sliding to his left and on command again executing the left *shoulder rip* technique.
- Repeat the drill until all drill participants have passed each other.
- The drill continues both left and right until all drill participants have had a sufficient number of repetitions. (When the drill is executed with the drill participants moving to their right, a right *shoulder rip* is executed).

Coaching Points:

- Instruct defensive linemen to maintain a good football position as they move down the line of scrimmage.
- Make sure the *shoulder rip* technique is executed properly.
- Instruct defensive linemen to drag the back foot behind the power foot.

Safety Considerations:

- A proper warm-up should precede the drill.
- The drill should progress from form work to brisk work.
- The coach should closely monitor the intensity of the drill.
- Maintain a minimum distance of three yards between linemen in the same row.

Variations:

- Can be used with linemen driving out of a stance before executing each shoulder rip technique.
- Can be used with linemen using a hand shiver.
- Can be used as a defensive end or linebacker drill.

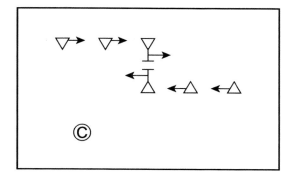

SLED EXTENSION DRILL

James E. "Jim" Carmody, Jr.
University of North Carolina, University of Mississippi, Buffalo Bills,
University of Southern Mississippi, Mississippi State University,
Mississippi College, Arizona Cardinals

Objective: To teach and practice the proper fundamentals and techniques of executing a forearm blow, with special emphasis placed on the hip roll. Skills related to reaction, agility, and tackling are also incoporated.

Equipment Needed: Two-man sled and footballs

Description:

- Position two rows of defensive linemen behind the pads of a two-man sled.
- A ballcarrier is placed five yards behind and on each side of the sled (see diagram).
- A manager sits on the sled and places a football on the ground between the pads of the sled.
- The coach stands between the two rows of defensive linemen.
- The first two defensive linemen line up in their stances, shading the outside of their front-facing pad.
- On the manager's cadence and ball snap, both defensive linemen drive into the sled, striking a blow with their inside forearm.
- Defensive linemen then recoil from their forearm blows and again assume their stances. This hit and recoil procedure is repeated two more times.
- After the completion of a third forearm blow, each defensive lineman executes a seat roll to the outside. Then they sprint and execute tackles on the ballcarriers, who are running for a position seven yards outside and to the front of the sled.
- The drill continues until all defensive linemen have had a sufficient number of repetitions both left and right.

Coaching Points:

- Always check to see that defensive linemen are in their proper stances.
- Insist that defensive linemen drive off the ball snap.
- Emphasize the importance of the hip roll in delivering the forearm blow.
- Make sure defensive linemen maintain the desired body position when contacting the sled.

- Make sure defensive linemen practice the proper fundamentals and techniques in executing all tackles.

Safety Considerations:

- A proper warm-up should precede the drill.
- Make sure that the drill area is clear of all foreign articles.
- The drill should progress from form tackling to full-speed tackling (not live tackling).
- Instruct the defensive linemen of the proper fundamentals and techniques of safe tackling.
- The coach should closely monitor the intensity of the tackling aspect of the drill.
- The sled should be checked periodically for possible maintenance and repairs.

Variation:

- Can be used with defensive linemen rushing the passer instead of executing the tackle.

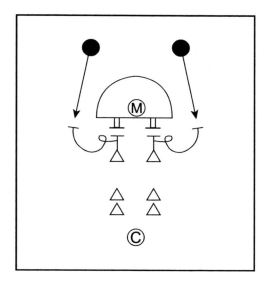

HEADS*

Mike Kelly
University of Dayton
National Champions: 1989
National Coach of the Year: 1989 and 1991

Objective: To teach and practice the proper fundamentals and techniques of reading and reacting to various blocking schemes presented to a noseguard by a center and two guards.

Equipment Needed: Flash cards

Description:

- Align a center and two offensive guards in their normal alignment on a selected line of scrimmage.

- A noseguard is aligned in his normal position over the center.

- Other noseguards stand adjacent to the drill area or may be used as offensive personnel.

- A coach stands behind the noseguard holding various center-guard blocking scheme flash cards.

- On the coach's cadence and snap count, the center and guards execute the designated center-guard blocking scheme that was shown on the flash card.

- The noseguard reads and reacts to the various blocking schemes executed by the center and guards.

- The drill continues until all the noseguards have had a sufficient number of repetitions.

Coaching Points:

- Always check to see that the noseguards are aligned correctly and are in their proper stances.

- In the teaching phase of the drill, the coach may alert the noseguards as to which blocking scheme the center and guard will execute.

- Instruct the noseguards to always keep their shoulders squared to the line of scrimmage as they read and react to the different blocking schemes.

---

* Reprinted with permission from *101 Winning Football Drills: From the Legends of the Game* by Jerry Tolley

Safety Considerations:

- A proper warm-up should precede the drill.
- Helmets should be worn and chinstraps snapped.
- The coach should place emphasis on the fact that this is a read-and-reaction drill and not a contact drill.

Variation:

- Can be used as an offensive center and guard-blocking drill.

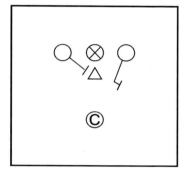

NOSEGUARD EXPLOSION DRILL

Jerry H. Moore
Southern Methodist University, University of Nebraska, University of North Texas, Texas Tech University, University of Arkansas, Appalachian State University

Objective: To teach and practice the proper fundamentals and techniques of defeating various center blocks. Skills related to pursuit are also incorporated.

Equipment Needed: Four large blocking dummies and footballs

Description:

- Align a quarterback and a center over the football on a selected line of scrimmage.
- Position a noseguard in his normal alignment over the center.
- Lay dummies in the neutral zone at the guard and tackle positions (see diagram).
- The coach stands adjacent to the noseguard.
- Other drill participants stand adjacent to drill area.
- On the quarterback's cadence and ball snap, the noseguard reacts to and defeats selected blocks of the center and pursues playside over and through the dummies.
- The drill continues until all participants have had a sufficient number of repetitions.

Coaching Points:

- Always check to see that the noseguards are aligned correctly and are in their proper stances (eye level of the noseguards should be the same as that of the centers).
- Make sure that noseguards use proper fundamentals and techniques of defeating the various blocks of the center.
- Instruct the noseguards to keep their shoulders squared to the line of scrimmage as they pursue over and through the dummies.
- In the early stages of the drill, alert the noseguards as to what type of block the center will execute.

Safety Considerations:

- A proper warm-up should precede the drill.
- The drill area should be clear of all foreign articles.
- The coach should watch for and eliminate all unacceptable match-ups of size and athletic ability.
- The drill should progress from form work to live work.
- The coach should closely monitor the intensity of the drill.
- Instruct the centers not to make contact with the noseguards after they initiate their pursuit over and through the dummies.

Variations:

- Can be used as a form or live block shedding drill.
- Can be used with a ballcarrier with the noseguards executing either a form or live tackle after pursuing over and through the dummies.
- Can be used as a center-quarterback ball-exchange drill.

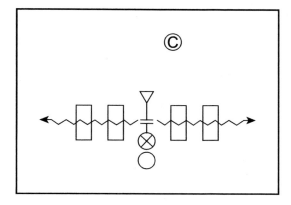

NOSEGUARD PURSUIT DRILL

Thomas W. "Tom" Dowling
Georgetown College, Liberty University, Cumberland College

Objective: To teach and practice the proper fundamentals and techniques of delivering a hand shiver, pursuing a ballcarrier, and executing a tackle.

Equipment Needed: Seven-man sled and footballs

Description:

- Align noseguards in a straight line in front of the center pad of a seven-man sled.
- Position ballcarriers in a corresponding position five yards behind the sled (see diagram).
- A manager stands on the sled with a football on the ground next to the middle pad of the sled.
- The first noseguard takes his stance in front of the middle pad and, on the manager's cadence and simulated ball snap, delivers a hand shiver to the pad. He then moves laterally down the sled delivering hand shivers to each pad as the ballcarrier begins to circle the end of the sled.
- After the noseguard has contacted all the pads, he circles the end of the sled and executes a tackle on the ballcarrier.
- The drill continues until all noseguards have had a sufficient number of repetitions.
- The drill should be executed with the noseguards pursuing both left and right.

Coaching Points:

- Always check to see that noseguards are in their proper stances.
- Insist that the noseguards deliver a good hand shiver to each pad.
- Instruct the ballcarrier to monitor his speed as he circles the end of the sled.
- Instruct the noseguards in the proper fundamentals and techniques of safe tackling.

Safety Considerations:

- It is imperative that a proper warm-up precede the drill.
- The coach should watch for and eliminate all unacceptable match-ups of size and athletic ability.
- The drill should progress from form tackling to live tackling.
- The coach should closely monitor the intensity of the drill.
- Instruct the ballcarriers to run well clear of the end of the sled.
- Make sure all noseguards use the proper fundamentals and techniques of safe tackling.
- The sled should be checked periodically for possible maintenance and repairs.

Variations:

- Can be used as a form or live tackling drill.
- Can be used for all defensive positions.

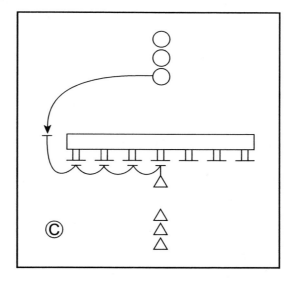

NOSEGUARDS TEACHING PROGRESSION

Victor E. "Vic" Gatto
Bates College, Tufts University, Davidson College

Objective: To teach and practice the proper fundamentals and techniques of reading, reacting to, and defeating a center's reach block.

Equipment Needed: None

Description:

- Align a center and quarterback over the football on a selected line of scrimmage.
- A noseguard is positioned over the center.
- The coach stands behind the noseguard, signals the snap count, and instructs the center to either execute a left or right reach block on the noseguard (see diagram).
- Other noseguards stand adjacent to drill area.
- On the quarterback's cadence and ball snap, the noseguard reads, reacts to, and defeats the block of the center.
- The drill continues until all noseguards have had a sufficient number of repetitions.

Coaching Points:

- Always check to see that noseguards are aligned correctly and are in their proper stances.
- Instruct noseguards to work for a position one yard across and to the play-side of the line of scrimmage.
- Instruct the noseguards to keep their shoulders squared to the line of scrimmage as they control the center's block with a forearm blow.

Safety Considerations:

- It is imperative that a proper warm-up precede the drill.
- The coach should watch for and eliminate all unacceptable match-ups of size and athletic ability.
- The drill should progress from form work to live work.
- The coach should closely monitor the intensity of the drill.
- A quick whistle is imperative with this drill.

Variations:

- Can be used as a form or live blocking drill.
- Can be used with center-guard combination blocks.
- Can be used with the various noseguard alignments and *shades*.
- Can be used as a center-quarterback ball exchange drill.
- Can be used as an offensive line blocking drill.

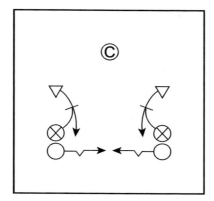

SHEDDING THE CENTER'S BLOCK

Robert A. "Bob" Pickett
University of Maine, University of Massachusetts

Objective: To teach and practice the proper fundamentals and techniques of reading, reacting to, and defeating selected blocks by the center.

Equipment Needed: Footballs

Description:

- Align a quarterback and center over the football on a selected line of scrimmage.
- A noseguard is positioned over the center (see diagram).
- The coach stands behind the noseguard, signals the snap count, and instructs the center to execute a specific block (drive block, reach block left or right, or pass block).
- Other noseguards stand adjacent to the drill area.
- On the quarterback's cadence and ball snap, the noseguard reads, reacts to, and defeats selected blocks by the center.
- The drill continues until all noseguards have had a sufficient number of repetitions against various center blocks.

Coaching Points:

- Always make sure that noseguards are aligned correctly and are in their proper stances.
- Instruct the noseguards to drive off the ball low and quickly and to maintain play-side leverage on the center.
- Instruct all noseguards to keep their shoulders squared to the line of scrimmage as they control the block of the center.

Safety Considerations:

- It is imperative that a proper warm-up precede the drill.
- The coach should look for and eliminate all unacceptable match-ups of size and athletic ability.
- The drill should progress form form work to live work.
- The coach should closely monitor the intensity of the drill.
- A quick whistle is imperative with this drill.

Variations:

- Can be used as a form or live blocking drill.
- Can incorporate one or two guards and have noseguards read, react to, and defeat down blocks, double team blocks, and combination scoop blocks.
- Can be used as a center blocking drill.
- Can be used as a center-quarterback ball exchange drill.

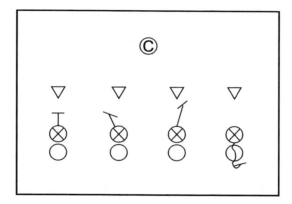

THREE-ON-ONE PASS RUSH DRILL

Herb W. Deromedi
Central Michigan University

Objective: To teach and practice the proper fundamentals and techniques in the execution of a pass rush against various blocking schemes.

Equipment Needed: Three large blocking dummies

Description:

- Position a center in his stance on a selected line of scrimmage.
- Align offensive guards in a post-snap pass block position two feet outside and two feet behind the center (see diagram).
- Stand three dummies eight yards behind the offense. (One dummy should be directly behind the center and the other two 10 yards on each side of the middle dummy.) The dummies represent various quarterback drop positions
- The noseguard is aligned in his normal position and is instructed to use a particular pass-rush technique (swim, rip, or spin).
- Other noseguards stand adjacent to the drill area.
- The coach stands behind the noseguard and signals the offense as to the snap count, pass action, and blocking scheme.
- On the coach's cadence and snap count, the noseguard reads the blocking scheme, executes the proper pass-rush technique, defeats the blockers, and sprints to the appropriate dummy.
- The drill continues until all noseguards have had a sufficient number of repetitions against various pass blocking schemes and quarterback drops.

Coaching Points:

- Always check to see that noseguards are aligned correctly and are in their proper stances.
- Insist that the drill be executed at full speed.
- Make sure that the noseguards read the various blocking schemes correctly.
- Insist that all noseguards execute the various pass-rushing techniques correctly.

Safety Considerations:

- It is imperative that a proper warm-up precede drill.
- The coach should watch for and eliminate all unacceptable match-ups of size and athletic ability.
- The drill should progress from form work to live work.
- The coach should closely monitor the intensity of the drill.
- The blockers should be instructed never to *cut block* the pass rushers.

Variations:

- Can be used as a form or live pass rushing drill (blockers can hold hand shields).
- Can incorporate a quarterback to execute various pass drops.
- Can be used as an offensive line pass-blocking drill.

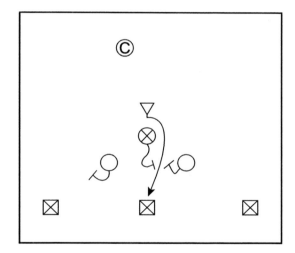

ATTACK AND REACT

Rayford T. Petty
North Carolina A&T State University, Southern University,
Norfolk State University, Howard University

Objective: To teach and practice the proper fundamentals and techniques of reacting to, attacking, and defeating four basic blocks: the reach block, the down block, the base block, and the pass set.

Equipment Needed: Football

Description:

- Position a defensive lineman in an outside *shade* alignment to an offensive lineman on a selected line of scrimmage.
- Position an alternating offensive lineman over the football at the center position.
- Other drill participants stand adjacent to the drill area (see diagrams).
- The coach is positioned behind the defensive lineman and signals the offensive lineman and center as to the block to be executed and the snap count.
- On the coach's cadence and ball snap, the offensive lineman executes the designated block (reach, down, base, or pass).
- The defensive lineman reacts to, attacks, and defeats the block of the offensive lineman.
- The drill continues until all defensive linemen have had a sufficient number of repetitions.
- The drill should be conducted from both the left and right.

Coaching Points:

- Always check to see that defensive linemen are aligned correctly and are in their proper stances.
- Stress the importance of the offensive lineman giving *good effort* so the defensive linemen can gain the greatest benefit.
- Emphasize the importance of being *quick off the ball* and using the hands aggressively.
- Make sure all defensive linemen practice the proper fundamentals and techniques of reacting to, attacking, and defeating the four basic blocks.

- In reacting to and defeating the reach block, emphasize the importance of not allowing the blocker to take away the defensive lineman's outside leverage. If the blocker is successful in taking away the defensive lineman's outside leverage, the *push and pull* technique must be used. (In using the *push and pull* technique, the defensive lineman should aggressively push the blocker's outside shoulder with the outside hand and simultaneously pull the blocker's inside shoulder with the inside hand. After getting the blocker's shoulders turned, the defensive lineman escapes the block by *ripping* his inside arm) (see diagram A).

- In reacting to and defeating the down block, instruct the defensive linemen to use the *friction* technique. (In using the *friction* technique, instruct the defensive linemen to step with their inside foot while *jamming* their inside hand to the rib area of the blocker and their outside hand to the blocker's hip area. When used correctly, the *friction* technique will allow the defensive linemen to automatically close down the gap while positioning them in the desired alignment to react to and defeat the trap or kick-out block) (see diagram B).

- In reacting to and defeating the base block, instruct the defensive linemen to use the *butt and press* technique to create a new line of scrimmage. (In using the *butt and press* technique, the defensive linemen must take a *power step* with the inside foot, followed by a *balance step* with the outside foot. Simultaneously, the defensive linemen must aggressively press the blocker away with their face, hands, and pads to gain separation. When pressing away, emphasize the importance of keeping the elbows down and the thumbs up) (see diagram C).

- In reacting to and defeating the pass set, instruct the defensive linemen to close the distance between themselves and the pass blocker as quickly as possible. Also stress the importance of getting the hands on the offensive lineman and executing the appropriate pass-rush technique (see diagram D).

Safety Considerations:

- A proper warm-up should precede the drill.
- The coach should watch for and eliminate unacceptable match-ups of size and athletic ability.
- The drill should progress from form work to full speed.
- The coach should closely monitor the intensity of the drill.
- Instruct all defensive linemen in the proper fundamentals and techniques of reacting to, attacking, and defeating the four basic blocks.

Variations:

- Can be used as a pre-game warm-up drill.
- Can be used with multiple paired drill participants reacting to, attacking, and defeating the various blocks.
- Can be used as an offensive line drill.

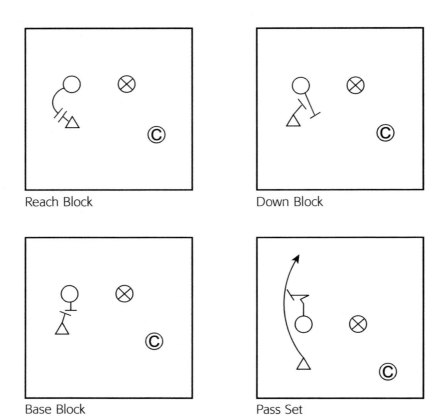

Reach Block

Down Block

Base Block

Pass Set

2

Defensive End Drills

BLOCK PROTECTION

Glen Mason
Allegheny College, Ball State University, Iowa State University,
University of Illinois, The Ohio State University, Kent State University,
University of Kansas, University of Minnesota
National Coach of the Year: Minnesota 1999
AFCA President: 2002

Objective: To teach and practice the proper fundamentals and techniques of reacting to and defeating high and low blocks.

Equipment Needed: None

Description:

- Position a defensive end in his normal alignment over the tight end.
- Align alternating defensive ends at the tight end position and in a two-deep alignment at the fullback position (see diagram).
- The coach is positioned in the offensive backfield, adjacent to the tight end.
- On the coach's cadence and snap count, the tight end simulates a down block and the two fullbacks move to block the defensive end.
- The defensive end reacts to the tight ends down block, and then focuses his eyes to the inside into the backfield.
- The first fullback executes a low block directed on the outside leg of the defensive end and the second fullback executes a high block, kicking the defensive end out.
- The defensive end reacts to and defeats both the low and high blocks of the fullbacks using the designated technique.
- The drill continues until all defensive ends have had a sufficient number of repetitions.
- The drill should be conducted from both the left and right.

Coaching Points:

- Always check to see that defensive ends are aligned correctly and are in their proper stances.
- Instruct the tight ends to drive hard and to stay low in executing the simulated down block.
- Insist that the defensive ends maintain a good *football position*, focusing on the helmet of the fullbacks and keeping the outside leg back and hands low in defeating both high and low blocks.

- Instruct the defensive ends to always expect the low block first and then the high block.
- Instruct the defensive ends, when defeating the low blocks, to push the blocks *out and away* using the hands.
- Instruct the defensive ends, when defeating the high blocks, to keep a squared-shoulder relationship to the fullbacks and to *rip* the inside forearm under the pad of the fullbacks.

Safety Considerations:

- A proper warm-up should precede the drill.
- Full equipment should be worn.
- The drill should progress from form work to full speed.
- The coach should closely monitor the intensity of the drill.
- Instruct the defensive ends in the proper fundamentals and techniques of reacting to and defeating low and high blocks.

Variations:

- Can vary the number of blockers executing the low and high blocks.
- Can incorporate a ballcarrier for the defensive end to read and react to.

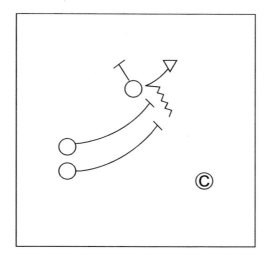

BASIC CUT BLOCK PREVENTION

Charles "Chuck" Amato
University of Arizona, Florida State University, North Carolina State University

Objective: To teach and practice the proper fundamentals and techniques of reacting to and defeating the cut block.

Equipment Needed: None

Description:

- Align a row of defensive ends (blockers) down on all fours on a selected line of scrimmage. Three yards should separate each of the blockers (see diagram).
- Position a defensive end in his *base* alignment over the first blocker.
- The coach stands adjacent to the drill area.
- On the coach's command, the first blocker drives from his stance and executes a cut block to the outside knee of the defensive end.
- The defensive end reacts to and defeats the cut block.
- After defeating the cut block of the first blocker, the defensive end moves down the line to the next blocker and readjusts his base alignment. The procedure is repeated until the defensive end has reacted to and defeated the cut blocks of all the down blockers.
- The drill continues as the performing defensive end assumes the position as a blocker at the end of the line, and the first blocker now assumes the position of the performing defensive end.
- The drill continues until all defensive ends have had a sufficient number of repetitions.
- The drill should be conducted from both the left and right.

Coaching Points:

- Always check to see that defensive ends are aligned correctly and are in their proper stances.
- Instruct the defensive ends to keep their eyes on the blocker until the block is defeated.
- Emphasize the importance of pushing the blockers to the ground using the hands.
- Insist that the defensive ends always keep the blockers to their inside half.
- Instruct the defensive ends to always keep their outside arm and leg free.
- Make sure defensive ends use the proper fundamentals and techniques of defeating the cut block.

Safety Considerations:

- A proper warm-up should precede the drill.
- Full equipment should be worn.
- The drill area should be clear of all foreign articles.
- Instruct the blockers to never execute their cut blocks until the defensive end is completely set in his base alignment.
- The drill should progress from form work to full speed.
- Instruct all defensive ends in the proper fundamentals and techniques of defeating the cut block.

Variations:

- Can be used with blockers aligned in three-point stances.
- Can be used as a linebacker drill.

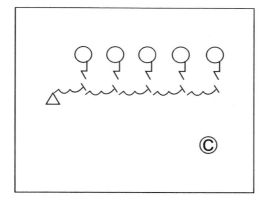

KEY DRILL*

James C. "Jim" Young
University of Arizona, Purdue University, United States Military Academy
National Coach of the Year: Army 1984
College Football Hall of Fame: 1999

Objective: To teach and practice the proper fundamentals and techniques of keying and reacting to the onside flow from the 50-defense.

Equipment Needed: Footballs

Description:

- Align a half-line offense (center, guard, tackle, tight end, and I backfield) over the football on a selected line of scrimmage.
- A defensive end takes his normal position over the tight end.
- Alternating defensive ends stand adjacent to the drill area.
- On the quarterback's cadence and ball snap, the offense executes one of five blocking schemes. The defensive end reads, reacts, and defeats the blocks of the different offensive players as shown in diagram. (A-tight end block, B-near back kick-out, C-offensive guard kick-out, D-running back kick-out, and E-tandem block.)
- The drill continues until all the drill participants have had a sufficient number of repetitions.
- The drill should be run with the offense in both left and right formations..

Coaching Points:

- Always check to see that the defensive ends are aligned correctly and are in their proper stances.
- Instruct the defensive ends in their read progression (tight end, near back, guard, and tandem block).
- Insist that the defensive ends stay low and follow their keys in the proper sequence.

* Reprinted with permission from *101 Winning Football Drills: From the Legends of the Game* by Jerry Tolley

Safety Considerations:

- It is imperative that a proper warm-up precede this drill.
- The drill area should be clear of all foreign articles.
- Full equipment should always be worn.
- The drill should progress from form blocking to live blocking.
- The coach should monitor closely the intensity of the drill.
- Instruct the offensive players never to cut block the defensive ends.

Variations:

- Can be used as a form or live blocking drill.
- Can be used to key and react from the split end side.
- Can be used with various offensive sets.
- Can be used as an offensive drill.

A
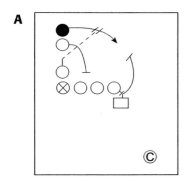

B
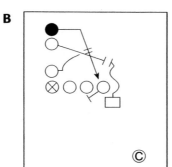

C
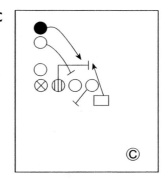

D
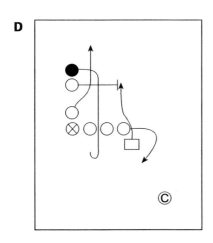

E
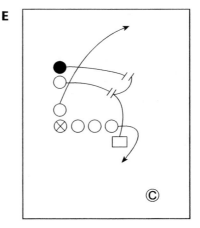

QUICK HANDS

John W. Thompson
University of Arkansas, Louisiana State University, University of Memphis, University of Southern Mississippi, University of Florida, East Carolina University

Objective: To teach and practice the proper fundamentals and techniques of using the hand placement on a blocker for leverage, block protection, and escape.

Equipment Needed: None

Description:

- Position a row of defensive ends (blockers) on their knees and with their arms resting at their sides on a selected line of scrimmage. One yard should separate each of the blockers.
- Position a row of defensive ends on their knees and with their arms at their side with finger tips touching the ground two yards in front of and facing the row of blockers (see diagram).
- The coach stands adjacent to the drill area.
- On the coach's command, the defensive ends (one at a time or in unison) strike a blow to the blocker's chest area just below the chest plate.
- The defensive ends then lock out their elbows, controlling the blockers with their hands.
- The drill is repeated in sequence three or four times in quick repetition.
- The drill continues until all defensive ends have had a sufficient number of repetitions.

Coaching Points:

- Always check to see that defensive ends are positioned correctly in a front-facing alignment.
- Instruct the defensive ends to always strike the blocker from the ground up, with the thumbs out and the elbows in and at their side.
- Emphasize the importance of focusing the eyes on the intended target, just below the chest plate.
- Make sure the defensive ends lock their elbows out as they control the blocker with their hands.

Safety Considerations:

- A proper warm-up should precede the drill.
- The drill area should be clear of all foreign articles.
- It is important that all drill participants keep their heads up during all phases of the drill.
- It is imperative that shoulder pads and helmets be worn.
- The coach should watch for and eliminate all unacceptable match-ups of size and athletic ability.
- The coach should closely monitor the intensity of the drill.

Variations:

- Can be used by having all drill participants standing and having the blockers jump forward to the defensive ends.
- Can be used by all defensive positions.

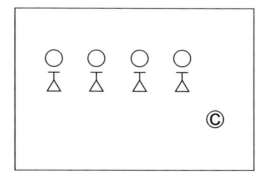

SPEED RUSH AND FINISH*

Chris Ault
University of Nevada
National Coach of the Year: 1978 and 1991
College Football Hall of Fame: 2002

Objective: To teach and practice the proper fundamentals and techniques of rushing the passer from the tight end side.

Equipment Needed: A quarter-inch rubber hose and a football

Description:

- Align a center, a tackle, and a quarterback in their normal positions on a selected line of scrimmage.
- Place a quarter-inch rubber garden hose in a circle (approximately five yards in diameter) adjacent to the designated line of scrimmage so that the back of the circle is at a point four yards behind the inside foot of the offensive tackle (see diagram).
- Align a defensive end at his normal position.
- Other drill participants stand adjacent to the drill area.
- On the quarterback's cadence and snap count, the offensive tackle executes his designated pass-protection block as the quarterback takes his five-step pass drop.
- The defensive end reacts to the snap count and drives past the block of the offensive tackle at the *intersect point* on the circle and strips the quarterback of the football (see diagram).
- The drill continues until all the defensive ends have had a sufficient number of repetitions from both left and right alignments.

Coaching Points:

- Always check to see that the defensive ends are aligned correctly and are in their proper stances.
- Instruct the defensive ends to lower their inside shoulder and to plant the outside foot as they accelerate through the block of the offensive tackle.
- Emphasize the importance of maintaining a tight corner at the *intersect point* of the circle.

* Reprinted with permission from *101 Winning Football Drills: From the Legends of the Game* by Jerry Tolley

- Instruct the quarterbacks to hold the football at different body alignments so that the defensive ends can practice stripping the football from various quarterback pass-throwing positions (above the shoulders and at the chest and waist areas).
- Insist that the defensive ends concentrate on the finish of the drill by first stripping the football from the quarterback and then recovering the football.

Safety Considerations:

- A proper warm-up should precede the drill.
- The drill should progress from formwork to full speed.
- Instruct the defensive ends not to hit or tackle the quarterback, but to only strip him of the football.
- When executing a live block with the tackle the rubber hose must be removed.

Variations:

- Can be used to read the draw and screen by inserting running backs and having the defensive end pursue the running back through the rush lanes for the draw and to the thrown football on screens.
- Can be used with the quarterback taking seven- and three-step pass drops by lengthening or shortening the diameter of the circle formed by the water hose.

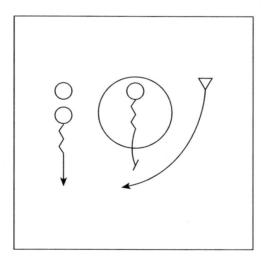

AIRPLANE DRILL

R. W. "Bob" Mazie
Southern Illinois University, Kutztown State University, Dayton University,
Southwestern Oklahoma State University, Arizona Cardinals

Objective: To teach and practice the proper fundamentals and techniques in maintaining leverage on the football.

Equipment Needed: None

Description:

- Align a tight end and two running backs at a 45-degree angle to a selected line of scrimmage (see diagram).
- Position a defensive end in his normal position over the tight end.
- The coach stands behind and outside the defensive end.
- Alternating defensive ends stand adjacent to the drill area.
- On the coach's cadence and snap count, the tight end executes a passive reach block on the defensive end.
- The defensive end reacts by stepping with his inside foot and defeating the tight end's block with a hand shiver.
- The defensive end then works his way upfield and defeats the passive reach blocks of the two running backs using the same hand shiver technique.
- The drill continues until all defensive ends have had a sufficient number of repetitions.
- The drill should be conducted both left and right.

Coaching Points:

- Always check to see that defensive ends are aligned correctly and are in their proper stances.
- Insist that all defensive ends maintain a good football position in executing each hand shiver.
- Instruct defensive ends to place one hand on the opponent's helmet and the other on his shoulder as they execute each hand shiver.
- Make sure the defensive ends shuffle upfield, keeping their shoulders parallel to the line of scrimmage as they take on each blocker.

Safety Considerations:

- A proper warm-up should precede the drill.
- The drill area should be clear of all foreign articles.
- Instruct defensive ends in the proper fundamentals and techniques of executing the hand shiver.
- The drill should progress from form work to live work.
- The coach should closely monitor the intensity of the drill.
- Instruct the blockers never to cut block the defensive ends.

Variations:

- Can be used as a form or live leverage drill.
- Can be used with running backs aligned in their regular positions.
- Can be used with pulling guards.
- Can be used as a tight end or running back blocking drill.

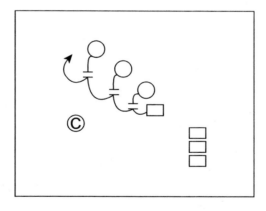

DELIVER A BLOW, FOREARM-HAND SHIVER, PARTS I–IV

Frank F. Navarro
Williams College, Columbia University, Wabash College, Princeton University

Objective: To teach and practice the proper fundamentals and techniques in the execution of the forearm-hand shiver.

Equipment Needed: Hand shields

Description:

- Align designated shield holders five yards apart on a selected line of scrimmage and instruct them to hold their shields with a firm grip and at a slight downward angle.
- A defensive end is positioned in his stance in front of each shield holder (see diagram).
- The coach is positioned behind the defensive ends.
- The drill is conducted in four parts as follows:
  - Part I. On the coach's command each defensive end extends forward from his stance (no step) and delivers a right forearm-hand shiver to a fit position on the shield. Three forearm-hand shivers are executed in sequence. The procedure is repeated with three left forearm-hand shivers.
  - Part II. Repeat Part I with each defensive end taking a step before extending and delivering the forearm-hand shiver.
  - Part III. Repeat Part II with each defensive end stepping, extending, and delivering the forearm-hand shiver, then slap stepping with the opposite foot. (The slap step is the follow-through with the opposite foot.)
  - Part IV. Repeat Part III with each defensive end gaining separation to the outside after the forearm-hand shiver is executed.

Coaching Points:

- Always check to see that defensive ends are aligned correctly and are in their proper stances.
- Make sure all forearm blows are executed properly.
- Instruct defensive ends to attain a good fit position on the shield.
- The defensive ends should control the blockers with their hand shiver.
- Make sure that defensive ends' heads are up and that their hips roll forward.

Safety Considerations:

- A proper warm-up should precede the drill.
- Insist that the shields be held properly.
- The drill area should be clear of all foreign articles.
- A minimum distance of five yards should be maintained between each pair of drill participants.

Variation:

- Can be used as a linebacker drill.

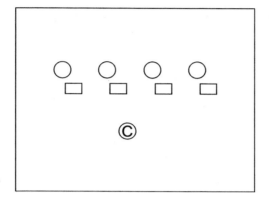

PRESSURE VS. VEER*

Robert "Bob" Reade
Augustana College (IL)
National Champions: 1983, 1984, 1985, and 1986
National Coach of the Year: 1983, 1984, 1985, and 1986
College Football Hall of Fame: 1998
Amos Alonzo Stagg Award: 1998

Objective: To teach and practice the proper fundamentals and techniques of defending the split-back veer-offensive set.

Equipment Needed: Hand shield and line marker

Description:

- Position a quarterback, center, tight end, and two running backs in their normal split-back veer alignment on a selected line of scrimmage.
- A line marker is placed just behind the hip of the offensive tackle position (mesh point).
- Position a defensive end, holding a hand shield, in his normal alignment over the outside hip of the tight end. (The hand shield will allow the defensive end to attack the mesh point and the quarterback at full speed and in a safe manner.) (see diagram.)
- Other drill participants stand adjacent to the drill area.
- The coach is positioned opposite the offense and two-yards behind the mesh point.
- On the quarterback's cadence and snap count, the offense runs the designated split-back veer play.
- The defensive end reacts to the snap count and drives through the *V* of the neck and shoulder areas of the tight end and directly to the mesh point.
- If the tight end reads inside veer, he continues straight down the line and attacks the quarterback.
- If the quarterback fakes the outside veer and drops back to pass, the defensive end redirects his charge upfield and pressures the quarterback.
- If the quarterback's action is away, the defensive end attacks him while looking for the bootleg.
- The drill continues until all the defensive ends have had a sufficient number of repetitions from both the left and right alignments.

* Reprinted with permission from *101 Winning Football Drills: From the Legends of the Game* by Jerry Tolley

Coaching Points:

- Always check to see that the defensive ends are aligned correctly and are in their proper stances.
- Instruct the defensive ends to first focus on the inside-veer mesh point and then the quarterback.
- Insist that the defensive ends drive through the *V* of the tight end and not to step around him.

Safety Considerations:

- A proper warm-up should precede the drill.
- The drill area should be clear of all foreign articles.
- The drill should progress from form work to live work.

Variation:

- Can be used to pressure a variety of offensive schemes.

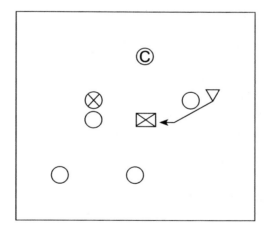

HIT AND PURSUIT DRILL

William "Bill" Robert Davis
South Carolina State University, Tennessee State University,
Johnson C. Smith University, Savannah State University
National Black College Coach of the Year: South Carolina State University 1981
National Black College Coach of the Year: Savannah State University 1989

Objective: To teach and practice the proper fundamentals and techniques of pursuit and tackling.

Equipment Needed: Three large blocking dummies

Description:

- Align a half-line offense (center, guard, tackle, tight end, and "I" backfield) over the football on a selected line of scrimmage.
- A defensive end lines up in his normal position over the tight end.
- Three blocking dummies are placed perpendicular to the line of scrimmage and five yards outside the defensive end. One yard separates each dummy (see diagram).
- Other defensive ends stand adjacent to the drill area.
- The coach is positioned two yards behind the first dummy.
- On the quarterback's cadence and ball snap, the offense executes the sweep play.
- The defensive end reacts to and defeats the reach block of the tight end. He then pursues over and through the dummies, and executes a form tackle on the tailback.
- The drill continues until alternating defensive ends have had a sufficient number of repetitions.
- The drill should be conducted both left and right.

Coaching Points:

- Always check to see that defensive ends are aligned correctly and are in their proper stances.
- Make sure that the defensive ends use the desired technique in defeating the tight end's reach block.
- Insist that the defensive ends maintain a squared shoulder relationship to the line of scrimmage as they shuttle over and through the dummies.
- Instruct the defensive ends to practice the proper fundamentals and techniques of safe tackling.

Safety Considerations:

- A proper warm-up should precede the drill.
- The drill area should be clear of all foreign articles.
- Instruct all defensive ends in the proper fundamentals and techniques of safe tackling.

Variations:

- Can be used as a form tackling or live tackling drill.
- Can incorporate a defensive tackle and have both the tackles and defensive ends defeat their blocks and pursue over and through the dummies.

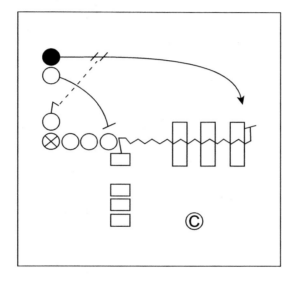

OPEN FIELD TACKLING

Corky Nelson
Baylor University, University of North Texas, University of Mary Hardin-Baylor

Objective: To teach and practice the proper fundamentals and techniques in the execution of an open-field tackle.

Equipment Needed: Six cones and a football

Description:

- Align cones in parallel lines to form a running alley 10 yards long and five yards wide (see diagram).
- Position a line of ballcarriers behind one of the rows of cones.
- Align defensive ends in a straight line in corresponding positions to the ballcarriers.
- On the coach's command, the first ballcarrier enters the running lane and attempts to run the alley.
- Also on the coach's command, the first defensive end enters the alley and either executes the tackle or forces the runner out of bounds.
- The drill continues until all defensive ends have executed a sufficient number of tackles.
- The drill should be run with ballcarriers and defensive ends entering the running alley from both the left and right side of the cones.

Coaching Points:

- Instruct the defensive ends to approach the ballcarrier from an inside-out relationship as they enter the running alley.
- Make sure the defensive ends practice the proper fundamentals and techniques of safe tackling.
- Instruct the tacklers to keep their heads up with eyes focused on the waist of the ballcarrier.

Safety Considerations:

- It is imperative that a proper warm-up precede the drill.
- Instruct all defensive ends in the proper fundamentals and techniques of safe tackling.
- The drill should progress from form tackling to live tackling.
- The coach should closely monitor the intensity of the drill.
- Instruct the ballcarriers that they should never try to run directly over the defensive ends.
- The training staff should be placed on special alert.
- A quick whistle is imperative with this drill.

Variations:

- Can be used as a form or live tackling drill.
- Can be used as a linebacker and defensive back drill.
- Can be used as a running back drill.

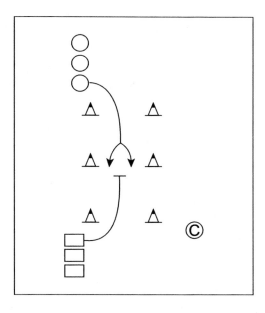

KEYING AND REACTING*

> ## Ronald "Skip" Schipper
> Central College (IA)
> National Champions: 1974
> College Football Hall of Fame: 2000
> AFCA President: 1994

Objective: To teach and practice the proper fundamentals and techniques of keying and reacting to various blocking schemes from the 50-defense.

Equipment Needed: Football

Description:

- Align a half-line offense (center, guard, tackle, tight end, and a designated backfield) in their normal positions on a selected line of scrimmage.
- Align a defensive end in his normal position over the tight end.
- Other defensive ends stand adjacent to the drill area or may serve as offensive personnel.
- On the quarterback's cadence and snap count, the offense executes one of six blocking schemes. (A-drive block, B-cross block, C-guard kick-out, D-back kick-out, E-sweep block, and F-pass block. See diagram.)
- The drill continues until all the defensive ends have had a sufficient number of repetitions reading all blocking schemes from both left and right formations.

Coaching Points:

- Always check to see that the defensive ends are aligned correctly and are in their proper stances.
- Make sure the defensive ends follow their correct read progressions (the tight end, tackle, guard, and near back).
- Instruct the defensive ends to react quickly on the ball snap, to always stay low, and to read and deliver a forearm blow on the approaching blocker.

Safety Considerations:

- A proper warm-up should precede the drill.
- Full equipment should be worn and chinstraps snapped.
- The drill area should be clear of all foreign articles.

* Reprinted with permission from *101 Winning Football Drills: From the Legends of the Game* by Jerry Tolley

- The drill should progress from form blocking to live blocking.
- The coach should monitor closely the intensity of the drill.

Variations:

- Can be used against various backfield sets.
- Can be used as an offensive drill.
- Can be used as a weakside defensive end drill.

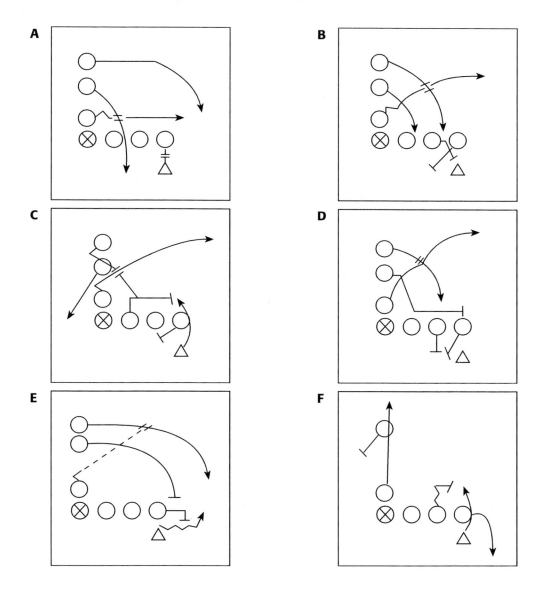

SHOULDER DRIVE DRILL

Oree Banks
Coahoma Community College, Grambling State University,
South Carolina State University, University of South Carolina, University of Virginia,
University of Wisconsin, Marshall University, West Virginia State University

---

Objective: To teach and practice the shoulder drive technique in rushing the passer from the split end side.

Equipment Needed: Footballs

Description:

- Align a center, guard, tackle, onside halfback, and quarterback over the football on a selected line of scrimmage.
- A defensive end is positioned in his normal split end alignment (see diagram).
- Alternating defensive ends stand adjacent to the drill area.
- The coach stands behind the defense and signals to the offense the snap count and one of three blocking schemes to execute (see diagrams).
- On the quarterback's cadence and ball snap, the offense executes the desired blocking scheme with the quarterback taking a seven-step pass drop.
- The defensive end reacts to the offense and executes the shoulder drive technique while maintaining an outside contain position on the quarterback.
- The drill continues until all drill participants have had a sufficient number of rushes from both the left and right.

Coaching Points:

- Always check to see that the defensive ends are aligned correctly and are in their proper stances.
- In using the shoulder drive technique, the pass defensive ends should direct their charge to the inside shoulder of the blocker. At the last instant they jab step and drive off the inside foot and redirect their charge through the outside shoulder of the blocker using a ripping action. In doing so, the pass rushers must convince the blocker that they are taking an inside charge.
- Instruct the defensive end to avoid contact when possible.

Safety Considerations:

- It is imperative that a proper warm-up precede the drill.
- The drill area should be clear of all foreign articles.
- The drill should progress from form work to live work.
- The coach should closely monitor the intensity of the drill.
- Instruct the offensive personnel never to cut block the pass rushers.
- Under no circumstances should the quarterback be tackled.

Variations:

- Can be used as a form or live pass rushing drill.
- Can be used in rushing the passer from the tight end side.

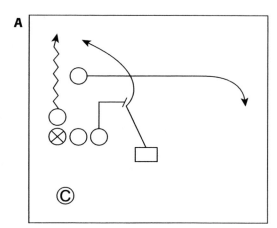

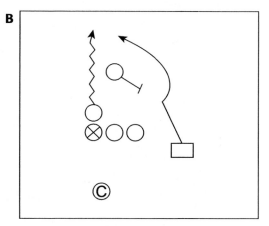

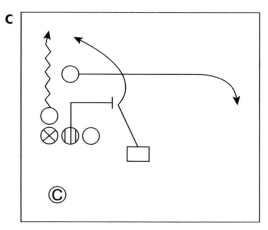

WIDENING

John L. Smith
University of Montana, University of Nevada, University of Wyoming,
Washington State University, University of Idaho, Utah State University,
University of Louisville, Michigan State University

Objective: To teach and practice the proper fundamentals and techniques in maintaining leverage on the football.

Equipment Needed: None

Description:

- Align three blockers two to three yards apart and at a 45-degree angle to a selected line of scrimmage (see diagram).
- A defensive end is positioned in his normal position over the first blocker.
- Other drill participants stand adjacent to drill area.
- On the coach's command, the blockers try to reach-block or cut-block the defensive end. The three blockers coordinate their blocks (reach, cut, reach or cut, reach, cut, etc.).
- In turn, the defensive end takes on and defeats each block while maintaining an outside leverage.
- The drill continues until all defensive ends have had a sufficient number of repetitions.
- The drill should be conducted both left and right.

Coaching Points:

- Always check to see that defensive ends are aligned correctly and are in their proper stances.
- Instruct the defensive ends to defeat low blocks with hand shivers and high blocks with a shoulder and forearm blow.
- Make sure defensive ends maintain a squared-shoulder relationship to the line of scrimmage as they defeat each blocker.
- The defensive ends must shed all blocks to the inside.

Safety Considerations:

- A proper warm-up should precede the drill.
- The drill area should be clear of all foreign articles.
- The drill should progress from form work to live work.
- The coach should closely monitor the intensity of the drill.
- Instruct blockers never to execute full speed cut blocks.

Variations:

- Can be used as a form or live leverage drill.
- Can be used with the three blockers aligned perpendicular to the line of scrimmage.

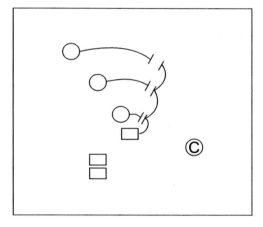

GET-OFF DRILL

Houston Nutt
Oklahoma State University, Murray State University,
Boise State University, University of Arkansas
National Coach of the Year: Murray State 1995; Arkansas 1999

Objective: To teach and practice the proper fundamentals and techniques of executing an aggressive get-off in rushing the passer.

Equipment Needed: Tennis ball

Description:

- Align a row of defensive ends in a straight line perpendicular to a selected line of scrimmage.
- A coach, holding a tennis ball, is positioned five yards in front of the row of defensive ends (see diagram).
- On the coach's command, the first defensive end assumes the designated pass rush stance.
- The coach then drops the tennis ball from eye level.
- The defensive end reacts to the dropped tennis ball, drives out of his stance, and attempts to catch the tennis ball before it bounces twice.
- The drill continues until all defensive ends have had a sufficient number of repetitions.

Coaching Points:

- Always check to see that defensive ends are in their proper pass rush stances.
- Instruct the defensive ends to drive out of their stances and accelerate to the dropped tennis ball.
- Depending on the surface, the coach should adjust the height from which he drops the tennis ball.

Safety Considerations:

- A proper warm-up should precede the drill.
- The coach should drop the tennis ball either to his left or right side to avoid contact with the on-rushing defensive end.

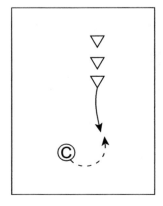

3

Linebacker Drills

HAT AND HAND BLOCK PROTECTION

Nick L. Saban
Kent State University, Syracuse University, University of West Virginia,
The Ohio State University, United States Naval Academy,
Houston Oilers, University of Toledo, Cleveland Browns,
Michigan State University, Louisiana State University
National Champions: Louisiana State University 2003
National Coach of the Year: Louisiana State University 2003

Objective: To teach and practice the proper fundamentals and techniques of reacting to and defeating the zone block.

Equipment Needed: Two cones

Description:

- Place two cones five yards apart on a selected line of scrimmage.
- Position an offensive lineman in a three-point stance midway between and three yards behind the pair of cones.
- Align a linebacker in the *ready position* six yards in front of the offensive lineman (see diagram).
- Other drill participants should stand adjacent to the drill area.
- The coach is positioned on either side of the cone area.
- On the coach's command, the offensive lineman drives either left or right out of his stance and executes a zone block on the linebacker.
- The linebacker reacts to and defeats the zone block of the offensive lineman using the designated technique.
- The drill continues until all linebackers have had a sufficient number or repetitions.

Coaching Points:

- Always check to see that linebackers are in their proper stances.
- Instruct the linebackers to maximize their power and strength by leading with the head and near leg, followed by the hands.
- Instruct the linebackers to make contact on the rise.
- Emphasize that the linebacker's head placement should be inside the blocker's breastplate with their thumbs up and *grabbing cloth* with the full extension of the arms.
- Stress the importance of accelerating the feet in contacting the block.

Safety Considerations:

- A proper warm-up should precede the drill.
- The drill area should be clear of all foreign articles.
- Full equipment should be worn.
- Make sure all linebackers use the proper fundamentals and techniques in reacting to and defeating the zone block.

Variations:

- Can be used as an offensive lineman drill.
- Can be used in reacting to and defeating the cut block.

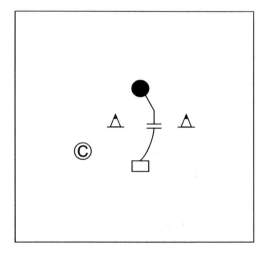

STRIKE, SHED, AND TACKLE

Al E. Seagraves
Shippensburg University, United State Military Academy,
University of Central Florida, The Citadel, Elon University

Objective: To teach and practice the proper fundamentals and techniques of delivering a forearm-shoulder blow, shedding the blocker, and executing the perfect form tackle.

Equipment Needed: Football

Description:

- Position four linebackers (blockers) in a two-staggered row alignment, with one yard separating the blockers from one another in both width and depth (see diagram).
- A fifth linebacker (ballcarrier) is aligned five yards behind the two rows of staggered blockers.
- Align a linebacker five yards in front of the two-staggered rows of blockers (see diagram).
- The coach is positioned adjacent to the drill area.
- On the coach's command, the linebacker reacts to and sheds the block of the first blocker. He then turns, reacts to, and sheds the block of the second blocker on his right.
- After reacting to and shedding the blocks of all four blockers, the linebacker executes the perfect form tackle on the ballcarrier.
- The drill continues until all linebackers have had a sufficient number of repetitions.

Coaching Points:

- Always check to see that linebackers are aligned in their proper stances.
- Instruct all linebackers to shed the block of the blocker using a forearm-shoulder blow.
- Insist that linebackers step up and make contact with the blocker with the same foot, forearm, and shoulder as they shed the blocks of the blockers.
- Instruct the blockers to avoid initiating their blocks on the linebackers until the linebacker has completely reset from the block of the previous blocker.
- Emphasize the importance of gaining separation on contact (with no wasted motion), and of keeping the feet moving.
- Make sure all linebackers practice the proper fundamentals and techniques of executing a forearm-shoulder blow, shedding a blocker, and executing a safe form tackle.

Safety Considerations:

- A proper warm-up should precede the drill.
- The drill area should be clear of all foreign articles.
- Full equipment should be worn.
- The coach should closely monitor the intensity of the drill.
- Instruct all linebackers in the proper fundamentals and techniques of delivering a forearm shoulder blow, shedding the blocker, and executing a safe form tackle.

Variations:

- Can be used with all defensive positions.
- Can incorporate a *hand shiver* and a *skate* technique in shedding the block.
- Can vary the distance between the linebacker, blockers, and ballcarrier.

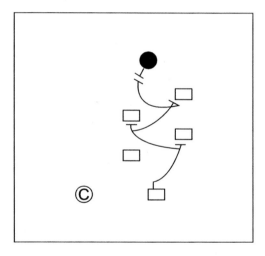

LINEBACKER REACTION

Tommy P. Bowden
Florida State University, Duke University, University of Alabama,
University of Kentucky, Auburn University, Tulane University, Clemson University

Objective: To teach and practice the proper fundamentals of breaking out of a pass drop.

Equipment Needed: Football and four cones

Description:

- Place four cones 10 yards apart to form a square.
- Align a linebacker in the *football position* midway between the cones at the front of the square.
- The coach, holding a football, is positioned five yards in front of the linebacker.
- Other linebackers should stand adjacent to the drill area.
- On the coach's signal (pointing the football), the coach directs the linebacker to execute a pass drop to one of the two back cones.
- After the linebacker completes his break to the designated cone, the coach redirects the linebacker's movement by pointing the football to another cone.
- The drill continues with the linebacker reacting to and breaking toward cones as signaled by the coach.
- The drill ends with the coach signaling the linebacker to sprint through the front two cones.

Coaching Points:

- Always check to see that linebackers are in their proper stance.
- Instruct the linebackers to open their hips and stay low as they react to the coach's signal and move from one cone to another.
- Insist that the linebackers keep their eyes on the coach throughout the drill.
- In an effort to improve agility and reaction time, the coach should always randomly signal the different directions of the linebackers' movements.
- Emphasize the importance of finishing the drill by sprinting through the two front cones.

Safety Considerations:

- A proper warm-up should precede the drill.
- The drill area should be clear of all foreign articles.
- Helmets should be worn with chinstraps snapped.

Variations:

- Can be used as a general agility drill.
- Can incorporate the *scoop and score* by fumbling the football on the ground as the linebacker sprints through the two front cones.
- Can be used as a defensive back drill (with the defensive back beginning the drill with a backpedal).

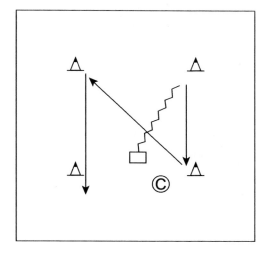

BREAK ON BALL*

Patrick Fain "Pat" Dye
East Carolina University, University of Wyoming, Auburn University
National Coach of the Year: Auburn 1983

Objective: To teach and practice the proper fundamentals and techniques of taking the proper pass drop, reading the quarterback, breaking on the football, and intercepting the pass.

Equipment Needed: Three footballs

Description:

- Align a quarterback (coach) holding a football at the midpoint of a selected line of scrimmage.
- Position a row of receivers one yard outside the hash mark and perpendicular to the line of scrimmage.
- A linebacker is placed in his normal alignment to the receiver side of the field (see diagram).
- Other linebackers stand adjacent to their drill area.
- On the cadence and snap count, the quarterback (coach) executes an eight-yard pass drop and passes the football to the wide receiver that is running either a 12-yard curl or a crossing route.
- The linebacker reacts to the snap count, executes his pass drop, reads the quarterback, and breaks on the football for the interception.
- The drill continues until all the linebackers have had a sufficient number of repetitions.
- The drill should be conducted both left and right.

Coaching Points:

- Always check to see that the linebackers are aligned correctly and are in their proper stances.
- Instruct the linebackers to set up simultaneously with the quarterback.
- Insist that the linebackers take the correct angle when breaking on the football.
- The passer should exaggerate his shoulder turn so linebackers will get a good read.

* Reprinted with permission from *101 Winning Football Drills: From the Legends of the Game* by Jerry Tolley

Safety Considerations:

- A proper warm-up should precede the drill.
- The drill area should be clear of all foreign articles.
- Instruct the linebackers to break in front of the receiver and to avoid all collisions.

Variations:

- Can be used with wide receiver running only the ending step of the patterns.
- Can be used as a wide receiver drill.

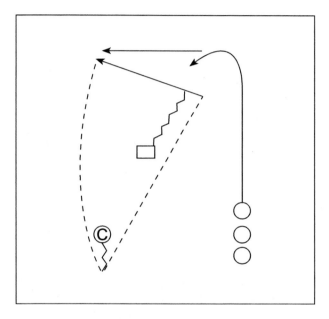

SCOOP AND SCORE

John S. Bunting

Baltimore Stars, Cleveland Browns, Rowan University, Kansas City Chiefs,
St. Louis Rams, New Orleans Saints, University of North Carolina
National Coach of the Year: Rowan University, 1992

Objective: To teach and practice the proper fundamentals and techniques of scooping up a fumbled football and sprinting for a touchdown.

Equipment Needed: Football

Description:

- Align a row of linebackers in a straight line perpendicular to a selected line of scrimmage.
- Position a coach, holding a football, five yards in front of the row of linebackers.
- On the coach's command, the first linebacker assumes the *football position*.
- At the coach's discretion, the football is fumbled on the ground.
- The first linebacker reacts to the fumbled football, scoops it up, and sprints for a touchdown.
- The drill continues until all linebackers have had a sufficient number of *scoop and score* repetitions.

Coaching Points:

- Always check to see that linebackers are in their proper stances.
- Insist that the drill be executed at full speed.
- Emphasize the importance of securing the football before running for the touchdown.
- After they scoop the football, insist that linebackers sprint for a designated distance before concluding the drill.

Safety Considerations:

- A proper warm-up should precede the drill.
- The drill area should be clear of all foreign articles.
- Helmets should be worn with chinstraps snapped.

Variations:

- Can be used for all defensive positions.
- Can be used as a fumble recovery drill (wearing full equipment).

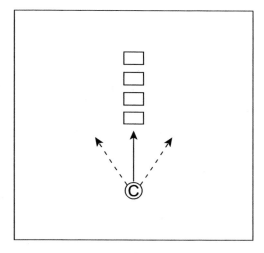

ANGLE PURSUIT

Sam Robertson
University of Tennessee, Kansas State University, University of Oregon,
University of Louisiana-Lafayette, Texas Tech University

Objective: To teach and practice pursuit. Incorporated are skills related to reaction, concentration, agility, and keeping a squared-shoulder relationship to the line of scrimmage.

Equipment Needed: Five large blocking dummies and two footballs

Description:

- Lay five large blocking dummies one yard apart on a 45-degree angle. Each dummy should be perpendicular to a selected line of scrimmage (see diagram).
- Position a row of linebackers adjacent to the first dummy.
- A manager is positioned at the end of the row of dummies.
- The coach stands in front of the drill area holding a football.
- On the coach's command, the first linebacker steps forward and assumes a *football position* beside the row of dummies. He then begins to shuttle over and through the dummies.
- At some point during the shuffle, the coach tosses the football to the linebacker.
- The linebacker catches the football, calls out *oskie*, and tucks the football under his arm. He then continues his shuttle over and through the dummies and gives the ball to the manager.
- The drill continues until all linebackers have had a sufficient number of repetitions.
- The drill should then be conducted with the angle of the dummies reversed.

Coaching Points:

- Insist that the linebackers maintain a good *football position* with their shoulders squared to the line of scrimmage and their eyes focused on the coach.
- Instruct all linebackers to pump their arms as they move over and through the dummies.
- Instruct the linebackers not to use cross-over steps.
- Insist that the drill be conducted at full speed.

Safety Considerations:

- A proper warm-up should precede the drill.
- Players with knee problems should be excused from this drill.

Variations:

- Can incorporate a ballcarrier and be used as a tackling drill.
- Can be used as a general agility drill.

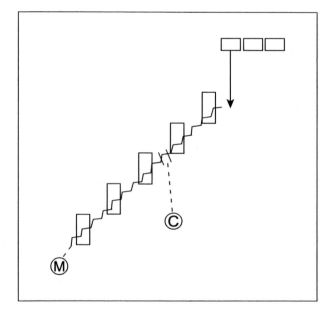

BASIC EFFORT DRILL

Donald J. Kelly
Elon University

Objective: To teach and practice the proper fundamentals and techniques of defeating both high and low blocks.

Equipment Needed: Four large blocking dummies

Description:

- Lay four blocking dummies three yards apart and perpendicular to a selected line of scrimmage.
- Position a row of linebackers in front of the first dummy (see diagram).
- Align a row of blockers in a front-facing position at the other end of the first dummy.
- The coach stands at the end of the dummy area and instructs the first blocker to execute either high or low blocks or a combination of the two. Linebackers are instructed to counter low blocks with hand shivers and high blocks with left and right forearm-shoulder blows.
- On the coach's command the first blocker drives out of his stance, straddles the dummy, and executes the designated block on the linebacker.
- The linebacker reacts to the movement of the blocker, straddles the dummy, and defeats the blocker with the designated block-shedding technique.
- The blocker and linebacker then retreat off the first dummy and the same procedure is repeated over the remaining three dummies.
- The drill continues until all participants have had desired number of repetitions.
- The drill should be conducted to the left and right.

Coaching Points:

- Always check to see that linebackers are in their proper stances.
- Make sure that all linebackers maintain a good football position during the entire drill.
- Insist that linebackers keep their shoulders squared to the line of scrimmage at all times.
- Always stress the importance of rolling the hips and *pad under pad* when executing the forearm-shoulder blow.

Safety Considerations:

- It is imperative that a proper warm-up precede the drill.
- The intensity of the drill should progress from form work to full speed.
- The coach should watch for and eliminate all unacceptable match-ups of size and athletic ability.
- The coach should closely monitor the intensity of the drill.
- Instruct all linebackers of the proper fundamentals and techniques of block shedding.

Variations:

- Can be used with varying distances between dummies.
- Can be used with any block-shedding technique.
- Can incorporate a running back and have linebackers execute a form tackle after defeating the last block.

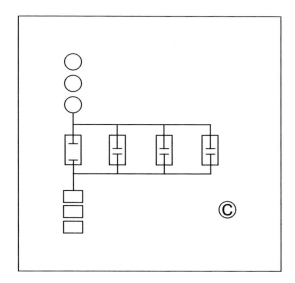

LINEBACKER TOSS-SWEEP PURSUIT*

Richard "Dick" MacPherson
University of Massachusetts, Syracuse University, New England Patriots
National Coach of the Year: Syracuse 1987

Objective: To teach and practice the proper fundamentals and techniques of filling the gap and pursuing on the toss sweep.

Equipment Needed: Two large blocking dummies and footballs

Description:

- Align offensive personnel (quarterback, center, two guards, tight end, fullback, and tailback) over the football on a selected line of scrimmage.

- Lay two dummies at the offensive tackle positions.

- Place linebackers and defensive ends in their normal alignments over the offense. (To emphasize inside linebacker play, have defensive ends hold hand shields.)

- Other drill participants stand adjacent to the drill area.

- On the quarterback's cadence and ball snap, the offense executes the toss sweep as the defensive personnel read, react, defeat blockers, and pursue the ballcarrier. (See diagram)

- The drill continues until all the drill participants have had a sufficient number of repetitions.

- The sweep should be executed to both the strongside and the weakside of the formation and from both left and right alignment.

Coaching Points:

- Always check to see that all personnel are aligned correctly and are in their proper stances. (Encourage linebackers and defensive ends to show blitz.)

- Instruct the playside linebackers to mirror the play, defeat the block of the onside guard, and pursue the ballcarrier.

- The backside linebackers are instructed to seal the playside *A* gap, defeat the cut block of the guard, and pursue the ballcarrier. (Caution backside linebackers not to get caught up in the line.)

- Insist that the linebackers maintain a good football position as they react and pursue each play.

- Make sure that all the linebackers react and pursue correctly on all plays.

* Reprinted with permission from *101 Winning Football Drills: From the Legends of the Game* by Jerry Tolley

Safety Considerations:

- It is imperative that a proper warm-up precede this drill.
- The drill area should be clear of all foreign articles.
- The drill should progress from form blocking to live blocking.
- The coach should monitor closely the intensity of the drill.
- Instruct the linebackers in the proper fundamentals and techniques in defeating blockers and executing safe tackles.
- Instruct the linebackers only to *thud up* on the ballcarriers.
- A quick whistle is imperative with this drill.

Variations:

- Can be used against the power sweep and other selected plays.
- Can be used as a defensive end drill.
- Can be used as an offensive guard drill.
- Can be used as a combination and team-play drill.

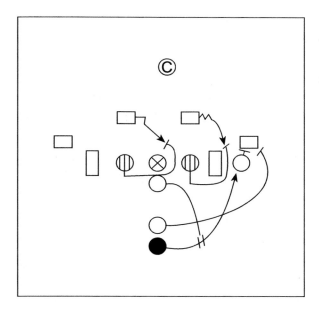

FIVE ON FIVE SHED OR AVOID

Robert "Bob" Giesey
University of Northern Colorado, Ripon College,
Ball State University, Grand Valley State College

Objective: To teach and practice the proper fundamentals and techniques of shedding a block and pursuing a ballcarrier. Also incorporates reading inside blocking schemes versus slant defenses.

Equipment Needed: Forearm pads (optional) and football

Description:

- Align an offense (center, two guards, two tackles, a quarterback, and a tailback) over the football on a selected line of scrimmage.
- Position a defense (nose guard, two tackles, and two linebackers) over the offense.
- Other linebackers should stand adjacent to the drill area (see diagram).
- The offensive unit breaks the huddle and runs plays according to a script as well as down and distance.
- The defensive line slants either left or right.
- The linebackers read and react to the various blocking schemes:
  - First series: First-and-ten plays
  - Second series: Second-and-six plays
  - Third series: Third-and-six plays
  - Fourth series: Third-and-long plays (passes, draws, and screens)
- The drill continues until all linebackers have had a sufficient number of repetitions.
- The drill should be conducted with the offense in both strong left and strong right formations.

Coaching Points:

- Always check to see that all personnel are aligned correctly and in their proper stances.
- Make sure that linebackers read and react correctly to the play being run.
- Instruct the offense to run only basic plays.
- Instruct the defense to run only angle defenses.
- Make sure that all linebackers practice the proper fundamentals and techniques of safe tackling.

Safety Considerations:

- It is imperative that a proper warm-up precede the drill.
- The drill should progress from walk-through to full speed.
- The coach should closely monitor the intensity of the drill.
- Instruct the offense to execute all blocks above the waist.
- Under no circumstances is this to be a live tackling drill (the tacklers should only fit-up on the ballcarrier).
- A quick whistle is imperative with this drill.

Variations:

- Can be used as a walk-through or a full-speed drill.
- Can be used as an offensive line blocking drill.
- Can be used as a defensive front drill.
- Can be used as a combination and team play drill.

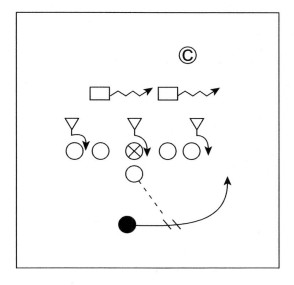

HIGH-LOW

Cally F. Gault
Presbyterian College

Objective: To teach and practice the proper fundamentals and techniques of defeating a block, pursuing the ballcarrier, and executing a tackle.

Equipment Needed: Four cones and a football

Description:

- Position an offensive guard in his normal position on a selected line of scrimmage.
- Place cones at the center, tackles, and other guard positions (see diagram).
- A running back, holding a football, is placed at the tailback position.
- A linebacker is placed in his normal alignment over the guard.
- Other linebackers stand adjacent to the drill area.
- The coach stands behind the defense and signals the guard and tailback of the snap count, direction of flow, and the type of block (high or low) to be executed on the linebacker. He also tells the linebacker the defensive front.
- On the coach's cadence and snap count, the offensive personnel execute their designated assignment.
- The linebacker reacts to and defeats the block of the guard, pursues the ballcarrier, and executes the tackle.
- The drill continues until all linebackers have had a sufficient number of repetitions.
- The drill should be conducted from both the left and right linebacker positions.

Coaching Points:

- Always check to see that linebackers are aligned correctly and are in their proper stances.
- Make sure linebackers' initial steps are in the direction of the backfield flow.
- Insist that linebackers practice proper fundamentals and techniques in defeating both high and low blocks and in executing a safe tackle.

Safety Considerations:

- It is imperative that a proper warm-up precede the drill.
- The drill area should be clear of all foreign articles.
- The drill should progress from form work to live work.
- The coach should closely monitor the intensity of the drill.
- The linebackers should be instructed on the proper fundamentals and techniques of shedding both high and low blocks as well as the proper fundamentals and techniques of safe tackling.
- Instruct the offensive guard not to continue to block the linebacker after the linebacker has initiated his pursuit.
- A quick whistle is imperative with this drill.

Variations:

- Can be used as a form or live tackling drill.
- Can be used with other linemen blocking on the linebacker.

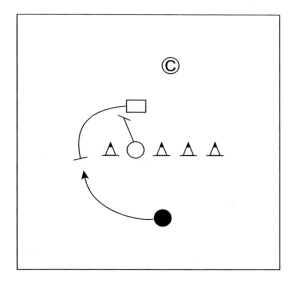

PURSUIT DRILL*

Dennis E. Green
Northwestern University, Stanford University, Minnesota Vikings, Arizona Cardinals
National Football League Coach of the Year: 1992 and 1998

Objective: To teach and practice the proper fundamentals and techniques of pursuing to the football, defeating a blocker, and executing a tackle.

Equipment Needed: Six large blocking dummies, two hand shields, and a line-spacing strip

Description:

- Position two linebackers in their regular alignments across from a selected line of scrimmage.

- Other linebackers stand adjacent to the drill area.

- Lay two large blocking dummies in the path of each linebacker's pursuit route (two-yards separate the blocking dummies). Two players, holding hand shields, stand adjacent to the dummy area. Stand another held dummy 10-yards behind each shield holder (see diagram).

- On the coach's command, the two linebackers pursue over and through the dummies, defeat the players with the hand shield, and sprint to and tackle the stand up dummy.

- The drill continues until all the linebackers have had a sufficient number of repetitions.

- The drill should be conducted both left and right.

Coaching Points:

- Always check to see that the linebackers are aligned correctly and are in their proper stances.

- Make sure the linebackers maintain a squared-shoulder relationship to the line of scrimmage as they pursue over and through the dummy area.

- Instruct the linebackers to fight through the hand shields and not to run around them.

- Insist that the drill be conducted at full speed.

* Reprinted with permission from *101 Winning Football Drills: From the Legends of the Game* by Jerry Tolley

Safety Considerations:

- A proper warm-up should precede the drill.
- The drill area should be clear of all foreign articles.
- Instruct all the linebackers as to the proper fundamentals and techniques of safe tackling.
- Instruct the dummy holders to release the dummies as the tackles are being executed.

Variation:

- Can be used as an offensive line blocking drill.

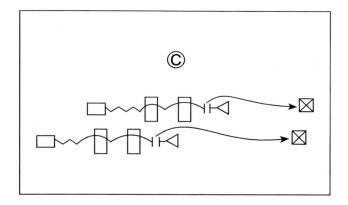

KEY DRILL

John Vogt
West Oregon State University, San Jose State University, University of Wyoming, Southwest Texas State University, University of Northern Colorado

Objective: To teach and practice proper fundamentals and techniques of reacting to and defeating a block and pursuing a ballcarrier.

Equipment Needed: Two large blocking dummies and a football

Description:

- Align an offense (center, two guards, two running backs, and a quarterback) over the football on a selected line of scrimmage.
- Lay two large blocking dummies outside the tackle positions.
- Position the linebackers in their normal alignment over the offense (see diagram).
- Other linebackers should stand adjacent to the drill area.
- The coach stands behind the defense and signals the offense as to the snap count and the play to be executed.
- On the quarterback's cadence and ball snap, the offense executes the designated play as the linebackers read and react.
- The linebackers are instructed to defeat the block of the guards using proper technique. They then shuffle into position to tackle the ballcarrier.
- The drill continues until all linebackers have had a sufficient number of repetitions.

Coaching Points:

- Always check to see that linebackers are aligned correctly and are in their proper stances.
- Instruct linebackers to always keep their shoulders squared to the line of scrimmage and never to use cross-over steps.
- Always check to see that linebackers are looking at and reading their correct keys.
- Make sure linebackers take on the guards with the proper technique and with their pads under the pads of the blockers.

Safety Considerations:

- A proper warm-up should precede the drill.
- The coach should closely monitor the intensity of the drill.
- This drill should never be conducted live.

Variations:

- Can be used with only one linebacker.
- Can be used as a block-shedding and form-tackling drill.
- Can be used to check linebackers' pass drops.
- Can be used as an offensive line blocking drill.

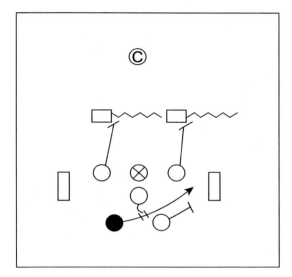

LINEBACKER ATTACK DRILL

Ralph Elliott Poss
Presbyterian College

Objective: To teach and practice the proper fundamentals and techniques of defeating blockers and pursuing through the trash in attacking the line of scrimmage.

Equipment Needed: Four large blocking dummies and a football

Description:

- Align four dummies at a 45-degree angle to each other and perpendicular to a selected line of scrimmage. One yard separates each dummy (see diagram).
- Place a blocker between dummies.
- A running back, holding a football, is positioned at the far end of the drill area.
- A linebacker assumes the *football position* beside the first dummy.
- Other linebackers stand in line behind the first linebacker.
- On the coach's command, the first linebacker *shuffles* over and through the dummies taking on and defeating each blocker with a forearm-shoulder blow.
- After the linebacker has moved over the last dummy, he executes a form tackle on the ballcarrier.
- The drill continues until all linebackers have had a sufficient number of repetitions.
- The drill should then be conducted with the angle of the dummies reversed.

Coaching Points:

- Insist that the linebackers maintain a good *football position* with their shoulders squared to the line of scrimmage throughout the drill.
- Insist that the linebackers use the proper block-shedding technique.
- Instruct the linebackers to execute all form tackles going upfield.
- Insist that the drill be conducted at full speed.

Safety Considerations:

- It is imperative that proper a warm-up precede the drill.
- Players with knee problems should be excused from this drill.
- The drill should progress from form blocking to live blocking.
- The coach should closely monitor the intensity of the drill.
- Instruct all linebackers in the proper fundamentals and techniques of block shedding and safe tackling.

Variations:

- Can be used with blockers on their hands and knees with the linebackers executing hand shivers.
- Can be used for all defensive positions.

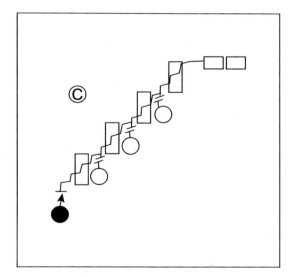

LINEBACKER BLOCK PROTECTION DRILL

C. F. "Rick" Taylor
Hofstra University, University, Lehigh University,
Dartmouth College, Boston University

Objective: To teach and practice the proper fundamentals and techniques of defeating blockers, maintaining outside leverage on the ballcarrier, and executing a tackle.

Equipment Needed: Three hand shields and a football

Description:

- Three blockers, holding hand shields, stand at a 45-degree angle to each other and perpendicular to a selected line of scrimmage. Three yards separate each blocker (see diagram).
- A linebacker is positioned in his stance three yards in front of, and slightly inside, the first blocker.
- Other linebackers should stand adjacent to the drill area.
- A ballcarrier, holding a football, is positioned seven yards in front of the linebacker.
- On the coach's command, the first blocker moves to block the linebacker as the ballcarrier initiates a controlled run to the outside.
- The linebacker reacts to and defeats the block of the first blocker and then in turn, reacts to and defeats the block of the next two blockers. He then executes a form tackle on the ballcarrier.
- The drill continues until all linebackers have had a sufficient number of repetitions.
- The drill should be conducted to both the left and right.

Coaching Points:

- Always check to see that linebackers are aligned correctly and are in their proper stances.
- Make sure linebackers maintain a squared shoulder relationship to the line of scrimmage as they move forward to defeat each block.
- Instruct linebackers to shed all blocks to the inside and to keep the outside arm and leg free.
- Make sure linebackers practice the proper fundamentals and techniques in executing the form tackle.

Safety Considerations:

- A proper warm-up should precede the drill.
- The drill area should be clear of all foreign articles.
- The drill should progress from half speed to full speed.
- The coach should closely monitor the intensity of the drill.
- Instruct all linebackers in the proper fundamentals and techniques of defeating blocks and executing safe form tackles.

Variations:

- Can be used with the ballcarrier cutting back to the inside at any time.
- Can be used with blockers executing either high or low blocks.
- Can be used as a form or live tackling drill.
- Can be used as an open-field tackling drill after the linebacker defeats the three blockers.
- Can be used as a defensive end drill.

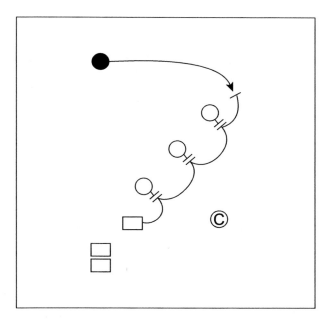

LINEBACKER ZONE PASS DROP DRILL

Timothy "Tim" James Rose
Miami University of Ohio, University of Memphis,
University of Cincinnati, University of Minnesota, Boston College,
East Carolina University, Eastern Michigan University

Objective: To teach and practice proper fundamentals and techniques in defending the number two pass receiver (tight end) from a pull-up pass action.

Equipment Needed: Five cones, four scrimmage vests, and footballs

Description:

- Place five cones to represent the five offensive linemen on either hash mark of a selected line of scrimmage.
- Place scrimmage vests in designated pass drop areas 10 to 12 yards deep on the sideline hash mark for boundary backer, eight yards over the tight end (hook zone), 15 to 18 yards over the tight end (seam area), and 10 to 12 yards deep on the field side hash mark (curl area).
- Position a quarterback, holding a football, and a tight end in their regular offensive alignments.
- Align the linebackers in their normal positions over the offense.
- Other drill participants should stand adjacent to the drill area.
- The coach instructs the tight end to run one of the four cuts (see diagram).
- On the quarterback's cadence and snap count, the quarterback executes his pull-up pass drop and the tight end runs the designated pass route.
- The linebackers react to the offense and follow these rules as they try to prevent the reception:
  - If the tight end hooks, the onside linebacker plays hook man-to-man and the backside linebacker drops down the hash mark 10 to 12 yards deep.
  - If the tight end runs a cross-under cut, the onside linebacker plays hook zone and the backside linebacker drops down the hash mark 10 to 12 yards deep.
  - If the tight end runs the seam, the onside linebacker plays the under seam cut to 18 yards and the backside linebacker drops down the hash mark 10 to 12 yards deep.
  - If the tight end runs to the flat, the onside linebacker plays curl, and the backside linebacker drops down the hash mark 10 to 12 yards deep.

- The drill continues until all linebackers have had a sufficient number of repetitions.
- The drill should be run from both the left and right hash marks.

Coaching Points:

- Always check to see that all personnel are aligned correctly and are in their proper stances.
- Make sure the linebackers read properly and carry out pass-drop assignments correctly.
- Instruct the linebackers to watch both the receiver and the quarterback as they execute their pass drops.
- Insist that the drill be conducted at full speed.

Safety Considerations:

- A proper warm-up should precede the drill.
- The drill area should be clear of all foreign articles.
- Helmets should be worn with chinstraps snapped.
- The drill should progress from a walk through to full speed.
- This drill is not recommended as a contact drill.

Variation:

- Can be used with other quarterback drop actions.

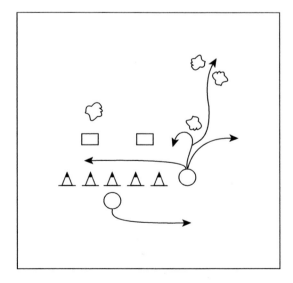

SHED TACKLE*

Bill G. Mallory
Miami University (OH), University of Colorado,
Northern Illinois University, Indiana University

Objective: To teach and practice the proper fundamentals and techniques of defeating a blocker, pursuing the ballcarrier, and executing a tackle.

Equipment Needed: Four cones and footballs

Description:

- Place two cones 10 yards apart on a selected line of scrimmage. Another cone is placed three yards outside the first two cones (see diagram).
- Position a blocker midway between the two inside cones. A ballcarrier, holding a football, stands eight yards behind the blocker.
- A linebacker is positioned four yards in front of the blocker.
- Other linebackers stand adjacent to the drill area.
- The coach stands behind the linebackers and signals the offensive players as to the snap count and direction of the play.
- On the coach's cadence and snap count, the blocker drives out of his stance and executes a drive block on the linebacker. The ballcarrier runs between the two cones as designated by the coach.
- The linebacker reacts to and sheds the blocker, then pursues and tackles the ballcarrier.
- The drill continues until all the linebackers have had a sufficient number of repetitions.

Coaching Points:

- Always check to see that the linebackers are aligned correctly and are in their proper stances.
- Instruct the linebackers to shed all blocks to the inside.
- Make sure the linebackers maintain a squared-shoulder relationship to the line of scrimmage throughout the drill.
- Make sure the linebackers practice proper fundamentals and techniques of block shedding and safe tackling.

* Reprinted with permission from *101 Winning Football Drills: From the Legends of the Game* by Jerry Tolley

Safety Considerations:

- It is imperative that a proper warm-up precede this drill.
- The drill area should be clear of all foreign articles.
- The drill should progress from formwork to live work.
- The coach should watch for and eliminate all unacceptable match-ups as to size and athletic ability.
- The coach should monitor closely the intensity of the drill.
- Instruct all the linebackers in the proper fundamentals and techniques of block shedding and safe tackling.
- A quick whistle is imperative with this drill.
- The training staff should be placed on alert.

Variations:

- Can be used as a form or live blocking and tackling drill.
- Can be used as a goal line drill.
- Can be used without blockers having linebackers pursue over and through dummies and execute the tackle.
- Can be used as an offensive line drill.

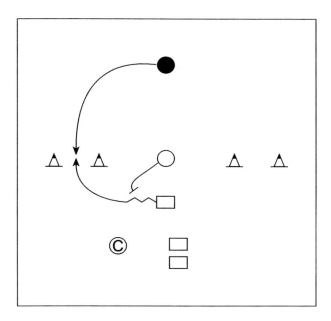

LOBO DRILL

Joe Lee Dunn
University of Tennessee-Chattanooga, University of New Mexico,
University of South Carolina, University of Mississippi, University of Arkansas,
Mississippi State University, University of Memphis

Objective: To teach and practice the proper fundamentals and techniques of defeating blockers, maintaining outside leverage on a ballcarrier, and executing a tackle.

Equipment Needed: Football

Description:

- Align three blockers at a 65-degree angle to each other and perpendicular to a selected line of scrimmage, with four yards separating each blocker.

- A running back, holding a football, is positioned behind the blockers (see diagram).

- Position a linebacker in a front-facing position 4.5 yards from the first blocker.

- Other linebackers should stand adjacent to the drill area.

- On the coach's command, the first blocker executes a high block and the second and third blockers execute roll blocks to the outside leg of the linebacker. The ballcarrier initiates a control run.

- The linebacker reacts to and defeats the first blocker with an inside shoulder blow and then uses his hand to avoid the second and third blockers.

- When the last block is defeated, the linebacker executes a form tackle on the ballcarrier.

- The drill continues until all linebackers have had a sufficient number of repetitions.

- The drill should be conducted to both the left and right.

Coaching Points:

- It is imperative that a proper warm-up precede the drill.

- The drill area should be clear of all foreign articles.

- The drill should progress from form work to full speed.

- The coach should closely monitor the intensity of the drill.

- Instruct all linebackers in the proper fundamentals and techniques of block shedding and safe tackling.

Safety Considerations:

- Always check to see that linebackers are in their proper stances.
- Make sure linebackers maintain a squared-shoulder relationship to the line of scrimmage as they move forward to defeat each block.
- Instruct the linebackers to watch the ballcarrier and to shed all blocks to the inside.
- Make sure linebackers practice proper fundamentals and techniques in defeating the three blockers and executing a safe form tackle.

Variations:

- Can be used as a form or live block-shedding drill.
- Can be used as a form or live tackling drill.

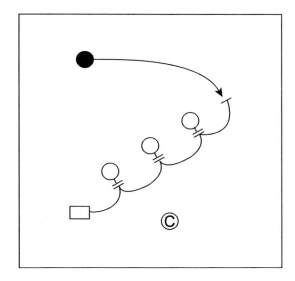

SHUTTLE BAG DRILL

Bill Yung
Texas Christian University, Baylor University,
West Texas A&M, University of Texas-El Paso

Objective: To teach and practice the proper fundamentals and techniques of maintaining a squared-shoulder relationship while pursuing over and through a row of dummies. Skills related to agility and concentration are also incorporated.

Equipment Needed: Five large blocking dummies and footballs

Description:

- Lay five large blocking dummies one yard apart and perpendicular to a selected line of scrimmage.
- Position a row of linebackers adjacent to the start area.
- The coach stands in front of the dummy area holding a football.
- On the coach's command the first linebacker begins his shuttle over and through the dummies.
- At some point during the shuttle, the coach yells "ball" and tosses the football to the linebacker.
- The linebacker catches the football and continues his shuffle over and through the dummies.
- The drill continues until all linebackers have had a sufficient number of repetitions.
- The drill should be run to both the left and right.

Coaching Points:

- Insist that linebackers maintain a good *football position* with their shoulders squared to the line of scrimmage as they shuffle over and through the dummies.
- Instruct the linebackers to always keep their eyes on the coach and to avoid cross-over stepping.
- Insist that the drill be conducted at full speed.

Safety Considerations:

- A proper warm-up should precede the drill.
- Players with knee problem should be excused from this drill.

Variations:

- Can be used by all defensive positions.
- Can be used as a general agility drill.

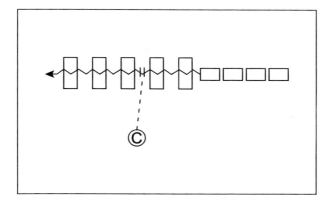

SLIDE TACKLE

Dr. Challace Joe McMillin
James Madison University

Objective: To teach and practice the proper fundamentals and techniques of pursuit and tackling.

Equipment Needed: Four large blocking dummies, two cones, and footballs

Description:

- Lay four large blocking dummies three yards apart and perpendicular to a selected line of scrimmage. Place a cone five yards in front and seven yards to the outside of both ends of the dummy area (see diagram).

- Position a linebacker in the *football position* between the two inside dummies. Other linebackers form a line behind the first linebacker.

- A running back, holding a football, stands five yards in front of the linebacker and between the two cones.

- On the coach's command, the ballcarrier initiates a controlled run around either of the two cones.

- The linebacker reacts to the ballcarrier's movements, shuffles over and through the dummies, advances to the cone area, and executes a form tackle on the ballcarrier.

- The drill continues until all linebackers have had a sufficient number of repetitions.

Coaching Points:

- Always make sure that linebackers are in a good *football position*.

- Instruct the linebackers to maintain an inside hip relationship to the ballcarrier as they move to execute the tackle.

- Make sure linebackers maintain a squared-shoulder relationship to the line of scrimmage throughout the drill.

- Instruct linebackers not to use cross-over stepping.

- Make sure linebackers practice proper fundamentals and techniques of safe tackling.

Safety Considerations:

- A proper warm-up should precede the drill.
- Instruct all linebackers in the proper fundamentals and techniques of safe tackling.

Variations:

- Can be used as a form or live tackling drill.
- Can be used with the ballcarrier changing direction.
- Can be used for all defensive positions.
- Can be used without a ballcarrier as a general agility drill.

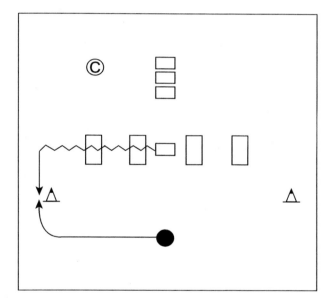

STOP THE CURL

Maxie Baughan
Cornell University, Georgia Institute of Technology, Baltimore Colts,
Detroit Lions, Minnesota Vikings, Tampa Bay Buccaneers, Baltimore Ravens

Objective: To teach and practice the proper fundamentals and techniques in executing the correct pass drop and breaking on and intercepting a pass.

Equipment Needed: Footballs

Description:

- Align a quarterback (coach) and two wide receivers, in the proper quarterback–wide receiver relationship, on a selected line of scrimmage.
- Position two linebackers in their normal alignments across from the offense (see diagram).
- Other linebackers should stand adjacent to the drill area.
- On the coach's cadence and snap count, the coach executes a straight drop back pass and the two wide receivers run designated hook or curl pass routes. The quarterback passes the football to the open receiver.
- The linebackers read, react, drop to their proper curl zones, break on the football, and intercept the pass.
- The drill continues until all linebackers have had a sufficient number of repetitions.
- The drill should be conducted from various positions on the field.

Coaching Points:

- Always check to see that linebackers are aligned correctly and are in their proper stances.
- Instruct the linebackers to always watch the quarterback and to work through the hook area to the curl area.
- Make sure the linebackers maintain a squared-shoulder relationship to the line of scrimmage as they move through their pass drop zones.

Safety Considerations:

- A proper warm-up should precede the drill.
- The drill area should be clear of all foreign articles.
- Helmets should be worn with chinstraps snapped.
- Instruct returning receivers to stay clear of the drill area.

Variations:

- Can be used with various pass drops.
- Can be used as a wide receiver drill.

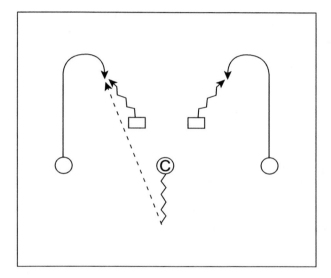

SPOT-LATERAL WAVE DRILL*

Jimmy Johnson

Oklahoma State University, University of Miami, Dallas Cowboys, Miami Dolphins
National Champions: Miami 1987
Super Bowl XXVII, XXVIII Champions
National Football League Coach of the Year: Dallas 1990, 1991, and 1992

Objective: To teach and practice the proper fundamentals and techniques in executing the correct pass drop and breaking on and intercepting a pass.

Equipment Needed: Footballs

Description:

- Align a defensive linebacker in his stance across from a selected line of scrimmage.
- A quarterback (coach), holding a football, stands five yards in front of linebacker. He instructs linebacker to execute a pass drop to either the hook or curl zone.
- Other linebackers form a line to the right of the coach (see diagram).
- On the quarterback's (coach's) pass drop, the linebacker moves to the designated pass coverage zone, works his feet in place, and watches the quarterback. As the quarterback looks and turns his shoulders, both left and right, the linebacker reacts and moves in the corresponding direction.
- The quarterback looks and turns his shoulders a final time and passes the football.
- The linebacker reads, reacts, and breaks on the football, intercepting the pass at its highest point.
- The drill continues until all the linebackers have had a sufficient number of repetitions.
- The drill should be conducted both left and right and from various field positions.

Coaching Points:

- Always check to see that the linebackers are in their proper stances.
- Instruct the linebackers to always open with the outside foot, to watch the quarterback, and to sprint to their designated pass coverage zone.
- Insist that the linebackers maintain a square-shoulder relationship to the line of scrimmage when they complete their pass drop.
- Instruct the linebackers to yell *pass* when they read the play, *ball* when the football is thrown, and *oskie* when they make the interception.
- Insist that the linebackers intercept the football at its highest point and sprint past the line of scrimmage after the interception is made.

Safety Considerations:

- A proper warm-up should precede the drill.
- The drill area should be clear of all foreign articles.
- Helmets should be worn with chinstraps snapped.

Variations:

- Can be used with various quarterback pass drops and linebacker coverages.
- Can be used as a defensive back drill.

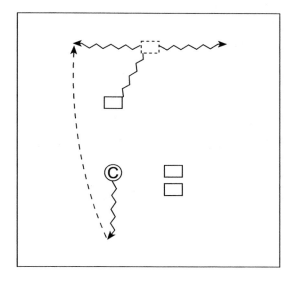

* Reprinted with permission from *101 Winning Football Drills: From the Legends of the Game* by Jerry Tolley

STRING-OUT

John B. O'Hara (Deceased)
Baylor University, Southwest Texas State University, University of Iowa

Objective: To teach and practice the proper fundamentals and techniques of defeating blockers, maintaining outside leverage on a ballcarrier, and executing a tackle.

Equipment Needed: Footballs

Description:

- Align two blockers and a ballcarrier at a 45-degree angle to each other and perpendicular to a selected line of scrimmage, with three yards separating each of the blockers and the ballcarrier (see diagram).
- Position a linebacker in a front-facing position three yards from the first blocker.
- Other linebackers should stand adjacent to the drill area.
- On the coach's command and in turn, the first blocker moves to execute a cut block and the second a high block as the ballcarrier initiates a controlled run.
- The linebacker reacts to and defeats the first blocker with a hand shiver, the second with a forearm-shoulder blow, and then executes a form tackle on the ballcarrier.
- The drill continues until all linebackers have had a sufficient number of repetitions.
- The drill should be conducted to both the left and right.

Coaching Points:

- Always check to see that linebackers are in their proper stances.
- Make sure linebackers maintain a squared-shoulder relationship to the line of scrimmage as they move forward to defeat each block.
- Instruct linebackers to shed all blocks to the inside and always to keep the outside arm and leg free.
- Insist that linebackers defeat the first block before moving to the second block.
- Make sure linebackers practice the proper fundamentals and techniques of shedding the blockers and executing the form tackle.

Safety Considerations:

- It is imperative that a proper warm-up precede the drill.
- The drill area should be clear of all foreign articles.
- The drill should progress from half speed to full speed.
- The coach should closely monitor the intensity of the drill.
- Instruct all linebackers in the proper fundamentals and techniques of block shedding and safe form tackling.

Variations:

- Can be used as a form or live block-shedding drill.
- Can be used as a form or live tackling drill.
- Can be used with additional blockers.
- Can be used as a defensive end drill.

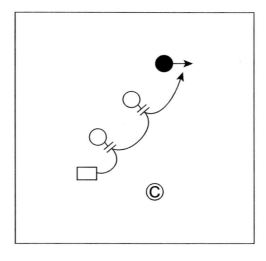

TRIANGLE DRILL

Dave McClain
Bowling Green State University, Cornell University,
Miami University, University of Kansas, The Ohio State University,
Ball State University, University of Wisconsin

Objective: To teach and practice the proper fundamentals and techniques in executing the forearm-shoulder blow. Skills related to reaction and teamwork are also incorporated.

Equipment Needed: Seven-man sled

Description:

- Position paired linebackers in their regular stances three yards in front of the pads of a seven-man sled. One pad separates the two linebackers (see diagram).

- Other paired linebackers form rows behind the first two linebackers.

- On the coach's command, the first two linebackers work their feet and execute a forearm-shoulder blow to the sled in one of the following three movement patterns:

  - Straight ahead: On the coach's first command, linebackers work their feet. On the coach's second command, the linebackers move straight ahead and execute a forearm- shoulder blow to the pad with the inside forearm. The linebackers then return to the starting positions.

  - Right: Linebackers continue to work their feet, and on the coach's command move to the pad on their right and execute a forearm-shoulder blow with the near forearm. The linebackers then return to the starting position.

  - Left: This procedure is repeated, with the linebackers delivering a forearm-shoulder blow to the pad on their left.

- After the three movement patterns are completed, the coach yells out and points either left or right. The linebackers react and shuffle in the designated direction to the end of the sled.

- The drill continues until all linebackers have had a sufficient number of repetitions.

Coaching Points:

- Always check to see that linebackers are in their proper stances.
- Make sure linebackers maintain a squared-shoulder relationship to the pads of the sled throughout the drill.
- The coach should instruct linebackers not to over-stride or use cross-over steps.
- Make sure all linebackers practice the proper fundamentals and techniques in executing the forearm-shoulder blow.

Safety Considerations:

- A proper warm-up should precede the drill.
- Helmets should be worn with chinstraps snapped.
- The sled should be checked periodically for possible maintenance and repairs.
- Instruct linebackers in the proper fundamentals and techniques of hitting a sled.

Variations:

- Can be used with linebackers positioned in front of different pads.
- Can be used with any number of varying movement patterns.
- Can be used as a defensive end drill.

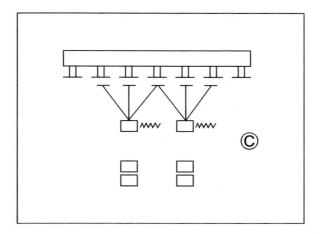

TRIANGLE DRILL*

Darrell K. Royal
Edmonton Eskimos, Mississippi State University,
University of Washington, University of Texas
National Champions: Texas 1963, 1969, and 1970
National Coach of the Year: Texas 1961, 1963, and 1970
College Football Hall Of Fame: 1983
AFCA President: 1975

Objective: To teach and practice the proper fundamentals and techniques of gaining separation from a blocker in executing a forearm-shoulder blow.

Equipment Needed: One large blocking dummy

Description:

- Align three linebackers in a football position in a triangle as shown in the diagram. One yard separates each of the linebackers.

- Lay a blocking dummy on the ground behind the linebacker designated as the defender. The two linebackers forming the base of the triangle are designated blockers.

- Other linebackers stand adjacent to the drill area.

- The coach is positioned behind the defender and signals the blockers either to come one at a time or in a predetermined sequence to block the linebacker.

- The defender reacts to and defeats each block with a forearm-shoulder blow.

- After the defender has executed a desired number of forearm-shoulder blows, the three drill participants rotate clockwise with another linebacker becoming the defender.

- The drill continues until all the linebackers have had a sufficient number of repetitions.

- The drill should progress from walk-through to half speed to full speed.

Coaching Points:

- Always check to see that the linebackers are in a good football position.

- Make sure that the defenders keep their shoulders low and squared to the blockers throughout the drill.

- Instruct the linebackers to take short jab steps as they move to defeat the blockers. After contact is made, the other foot should be brought forward.

- Instruct the defender to use their hands in gaining separation from the blocker.

Safety Considerations:

- It is imperative that a proper warm-up precede this drill.
- The drill should progress from formwork to live work.
- The coach should monitor closely the intensity of the drill.
- The coach should look for and eliminate all unacceptable matchups as to size and athletic ability.
- Instruct all the linebackers in the proper fundamentals and techniques of delivering a forearm-shoulder blow.

Variations:

- Can incorporate a tackling drill on a ballcarrier after gaining separation from the final blocker.
- Can be used as a defensive line and end drill.

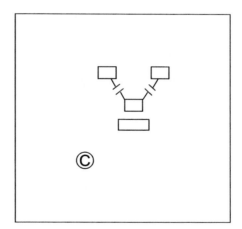

4

Defensive Back Drills

SIDELINE ANGLE TACKLING

Ron Zook
Murray State University, University of Cincinnati, University of Kansas,
University of Tennessee, Virginia Polytechnic Institute, The Ohio State University,
Pittsburgh Steelers, Kansas City Chiefs, New Orleans Saints, University of Florida

Objective: To teach and practice the proper fundamentals and techniques of executing a sideline tackle while taking away the threat of the ballcarrier cutting back to the inside.

Equipment Needed: Two footballs and two cones

Description:

- Place two cones 10 yards apart and seven yards from a selected line of scrimmage.
- Position a row of ballcarriers adjacent to and behind one of the cones, and a row of defensive backs adjacent to and behind the other cone (see diagram).
- The coach is positioned adjacent to the defensive backs.
- On the coach's command, the first defensive back begins his backpedal and then breaks back at an angle toward the sideline.
- The ballcarrier reacts to the defensive back's forward movement and initiates his run upfield and toward the sideline.
- The defensive back pursues the ballcarrier and executes the sideline tackle.
- The drill continues until all defensive backs have had a sufficient number of repetitions.
- The drill should be conducted to both the left and right.

Coaching Points:

- Always check to see that defensive backs are in their proper stances.
- Instruct the defensive backs to always stay behind the ballcarrier's running path, taking away the threat of the cutback. The defensive backs should use the sideline as a *twelfth defender* and give ground when necessary.
- Instruct the defensive backs to *come to balance*, keeping their head and eyes up before executing the tackle.
- Make sure all defensive backs practice the proper fundamentals and techniques of safe tackling.

Safety Considerations:

- A proper warm-up should precede the drill.
- The drill area should be clear of all foreign articles. This includes the sideline area.
- The drill should progress from form tackling to full-speed tackling (never live tackling). Never take the ballcarrier to the ground.
- The coach should watch for and eliminate all unacceptable match-ups of size and athletic ability.
- The coach should closely monitor the intensity of the drill.
- Instruct all defensive backs in the proper fundamentals and techniques of safe tackling.

Variations:

- Can be used as a linebacker drill.
- Can be used as a defensive end drill.
- Can be used as a form tackling or full-speed tackling drill (never live tackling).

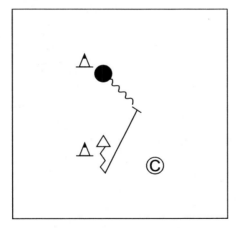

BALL-REACTION DRILL*

John H. Cooper
University of Tulsa, Arizona State University, The Ohio State University
National Coach of the Year: Arizona State 1986
AFCA President: 1992

Objective: To teach and practice the proper fundamentals and techniques of breaking on and intercepting a pass. Incorporated are skills related to agility and quickness.

Equipment Needed: Footballs

Description:

- Align a row of defensive backs 25 yards downfield from the midpoint of a selected line of scrimmage.
- A quarterback (coach) stands in front of the defensive backs and on the line of scrimmage.
- A row of receivers is placed perpendicular to the line of scrimmage and 10 yards away and on both sides of the coach (see diagram).
- On the coach's command, the first wide receiver in each line runs a post pattern.
- The first defensive back reads the quarterback (coach), breaks on, and intercepts the thrown pass. He then tucks the football away and sprints to the coach and hands it to him.
- The drill continues until all the defensive backs have had a sufficient number of repetitions.

Coaching Points:

- Always check to see that the defensive backs are aligned correctly and are in their proper stances.
- Instruct the defensive backs to always break in front of the receivers and to intercept the football at its highest point.
- Instruct the receivers that they are not to make the reception but can harass the defender by yelling or faking a tackle.
- Insist that the drill be conducted at full speed.

* Reprinted with permission from *101 Winning Football Drills: From the Legends of the Game* by Jerry Tolley

Safety Considerations:

- A proper warm-up should precede the drill.
- The drill area should be clear of all foreign articles.
- Under no circumstances should this be a contact drill.
- The coach should time his pass to ensure that there is no danger of the receivers running into each other.

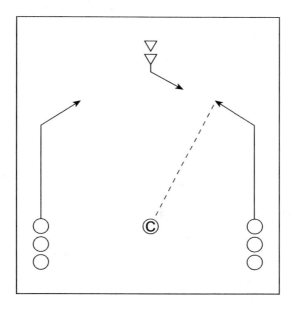

ANGLE TACKLING OR OPEN-FIELD TACKLING

Robert D. "Bob" Cope (Deceased)
Vanderbilt University, Southern Methodist University, University of Arkansas, University of Mississippi, Purdue University, University of Southern California, Baylor University, University of the Pacific, Kansas State University

Objective: To teach and practice the proper fundamentals and techniques of tackling. Skills related to agility, reaction, and quickness are also incorporated.

Equipment Needed: Four cones and footballs

Description:

- Form a diamond-shaped drill area by placing two cones five yards apart on a selected line of scrimmage and placing the other cones 2.5 yards in front of and in back of the midpoint of the first two cones (see diagram).

- Position a row of ballcarriers three yards from the placement of the front cone.

- Align a row of defensive backs in a corresponding position to the ballcarriers.

- On the coach's command, the first defensive back runs to the back cone and breaks down. When the defensive back breaks down, the first ballcarrier runs to his front cone and cuts either left or right and sprints downfield at a 45-degree angle.

- The defensive back reacts to the run of the ballcarrier and moves forward and executes the tackle.

- The drill continues until all defensive backs have had a sufficient number of repetitions.

Coaching Points:

- Instruct the defensive backs to break down, shuffle laterally, and keep an inside-out relationship to the ballcarrier.

- Make sure defensive backs make contact with the near shoulder and with their head in front of the runners.

- Insist that defensive backs execute all tackles on the rise with emphasis on the follow-through.

- Instruct the defensive backs in the proper fundamentals and techniques of safe tackling.

Safety Considerations:

- It is imperative that a proper warm-up precede the drill
- The drill should progress from form tackling to live tackling.
- The coach should closely monitor the intensity of the drill.
- The coach should watch for and eliminate all unacceptable match-ups of size and athletic ability.
- Make sure all defensive backs practice the proper fundamentals and techniques of safe tackling.
- A quick whistle is imperative with this drill.

Variations:

- Can be used as a form or live-tackling drill.
- Can be used with runners carrying hand shields.
- Can be used for all defensive positions.

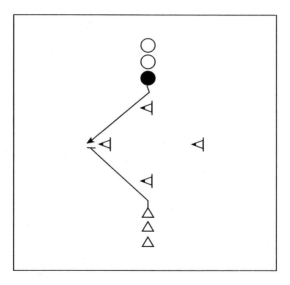

CONFIDENCE DRILL*

Carmen "Carm" Cozza
Yale University
College Football Hall of Fame: 2002
AFCA President: 1978

Objective: To teach and practice the proper fundamentals and techniques of covering the three-deep pass zone and intercepting a pass.

Equipment Needed: Footballs

Description:

- Position four rows of receivers at equal distances across the field on a selected line of scrimmage (see diagram).
- A three-deep secondary is aligned in its normal position over the receivers.
- The quarterback (coach), holding a football, is positioned at the midpoint of the line of scrimmage.
- Alternating defensive units are positioned on the sideline.
- On the cadence and snap count, the coach executes his pass drop as the first receiver in each row sprints straight downfield.
- The coach fakes one way and then passes the football to any one of the receivers as the defensive backs break for the interception.
- The drill continues until all the defensive backs have had a sufficient number of repetitions.

Coaching Points:

- Always check to see that the defensive backs are aligned correctly and are in their proper stances.
- Make sure the defensive backs keep both the receivers and the quarterback in their field of vision.
- Insist that the defensive backs always remain in their proper pass coverage zones.
- Instruct defensive backs to always intercept a pass at its highest point.

* Reprinted with permission from *101 Winning Football Drills: From the Legends of the Game* by Jerry Tolley

Safety Considerations:

- A proper warm-up should precede the drill.
- The drill area should be clear of all foreign articles.
- Instruct the receivers to always remain in their designated running lanes and to avoid all contact with the defensive backs.

Variations:

- Can be used with various quarterback-pass drops.
- Can be used with receivers running various coordinated patterns.
- Can incorporate linebackers.

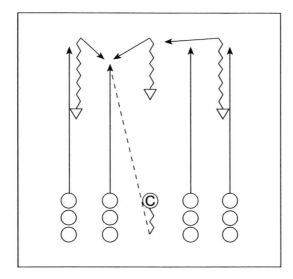

BACKPEDAL AND BREAK

George W. MacIntyre
Miami University, University of Tampa, Clemson University,
University of Tennessee-Martin, University of Mississippi,
Vanderbilt University, Liberty University
National Coach of the Year: Vanderbilt 1982

Objective: To teach and practice the proper fundamentals and techniques in executing the backpedal. Skills related to keying the quarterback, breaking on a thrown pass, and intercepting the pass are also incorporated.

Equipment Needed: Footballs

Description:

- Align a defensive back five yards across from a selected line of scrimmage.
- The coach, holding a football, is positioned on the line of scrimmage in front of the defensive back.
- Other defensive backs should stand adjacent to the drill area.
- On the coach's command, the defensive back begins to backpedal straight back. The coach then turns his shoulders either left or right and the defensive back reacts accordingly by breaking at a 45-degree angle and sprinting in the direction of the shoulder turn.
- The coach shows pass and the defensive back again goes into his backpedal.
- Finally, the pass is thrown and the defensive back breaks on and intercepts the football.
- The drill continues until all defensive backs have had a sufficient number of repetitions.

Coaching Points:

- Always check to see that all defensive backs are aligned correctly and are in their proper stances.
- Insist that all defensive backs keep a low center of gravity and execute their backpedal correctly.
- Make sure all defensive backs keep their eyes on the quarterback throughout the drill.
- Instruct defensive backs to break on the thrown pass at full speed and to intercept the football at its highest point.
- Insist that the drill be conducted at full speed.

Safety Consideration:

- A proper warm-up should precede the drill.
- The drill area should be clear of all foreign articles.
- Helmets should be worn with chinstraps snapped.

Variations:

- Can be used with defensive backs moving at angles to both the left and right of the quarterback.
- Can be used with the football thrown at varying trajectories and angles (45-degrees forward, 45-degrees backward, 90-degrees, etc.).
- Can be used as a linebacker and defensive end drill.

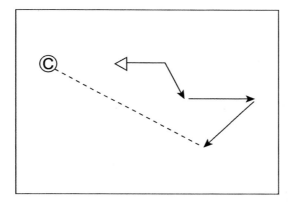

CUSHION DRILL*

T. C. "Chan" Gailey
Samford University, Troy State University, Birmingham Fire,
Dallas Cowboys, Georgia Institute of Technology
National Champions: Troy State 1984
National Coach of the Year: Troy State 1984

Objective: To teach and practice the proper fundamentals and techniques of cushioning a receiver. Can also be used as a warm-up drill.

Equipment Needed: None

Description:

- Position a row of wide receivers perpendicular to a selected line of scrimmage.
- Align a defensive back in his normal position across from the first wide receiver.
- Other defensive backs stand adjacent to the drill area.
- The coach will vary his position around the drill area.
- On the coach's command, the first receiver runs one-half to three-quarter speed straight down the field. The defensive back backpedals, keeping a designated cushion of two yards vertical and one yard horizontal on either the inside or outside of the receiver. If the wide receiver breaks the designated cushion, the defensive back will have to turn out of his backpedal and run with the receiver.
- The drill continues until all the defensive backs have had a sufficient number of repetitions both to the inside and outside of the receiver.

Coaching Points:

- Always check to see that the defensive backs are aligned correctly and are in their proper stances.
- Insist that the defensive backs execute their backpedal correctly.
- The coach should view the drill from various angles in order to check for the proper vertical and horizontal cushion.

---

* Reprinted with permission from *101 Winning Football Drills: From the Legends of the Game* by Jerry Tolley

Safety Considerations:

- A proper warm-up should precede the drill.
- The drill area should be clear of all foreign articles.

Variations:

- Can be used with receivers cutting left and right as they run downfield.
- Can be used with receivers running at full speed.
- Can be used with a quarterback throwing a pass to the receivers.

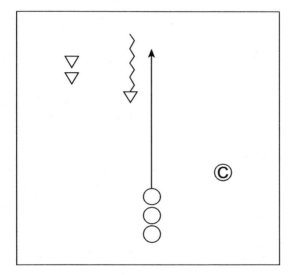

FOUR-POINT BREAKING DRILL*

Frank M. Beamer
Murray State University, Virginia Polytechnic Institute
National Coach of the Year: Virginia Tech 1999

Objective: To teach and practice the proper fundamentals and techniques of breaking on and intercepting the football.

Equipment Needed: Four large blocking dummies and footballs

Description:

- Position a defensive back at the midpoint of a selected yard line.
- The quarterback (coach), holding a football, stands 20 yards in front of the defensive back.
- Other defensive backs stand adjacent to the drill area.
- A dummy is placed 10 yards on both sides of the defensive back. Two additional dummies are placed 20 yards downfield and 30 yards apart (see diagram).
- On the coach's signal, the defensive back initiates his backpedal. When the defensive back has backpedaled approximately five yards, the coach will turn and throw the football (with long-arm motion) to one of the four dummies.
- The defensive back reads the long-arm motion of the quarterback and sprints to the football and makes the interception.
- The drill continues until all the defensive backs have had a sufficient number of repetitions.

Coaching Points:

- Check to see that the defensive backs are in their proper stances.
- Insist that the defensive backs execute their backpedal correctly keeping their eyes on the quarterback.
- Instruct the defensive backs to get a good plant off their backpedal and to take the proper angle to intercept the football.
- Make sure the defensive backs break through or in front of the dummy as they intercept the pass at its highest point.

* Reprinted with permission from *101 Winning Football Drills: From the Legends of the Game* by Jerry Tolley

Safety Considerations:

- A proper warm-up should precede the drill.
- The drill area should be clear of all foreign articles.

Variations:

- Can be used with dummies placed at varying positions on the field.
- Can be used as a linebacker drill.

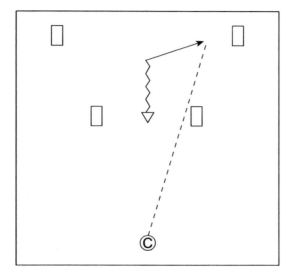

BALL DRILL

Jerry L. Stovall
University of South Carolina, Louisiana State University
National Coach of the Year: Louisiana State University 1983

Objective: To teach and practice the proper fundamentals and techniques of catching the football with special emphasis on concentration.

Equipment Needed: Footballs

Description:

- Align a defensive back facing the sideline at the junction of a selected yard line and the sideline.
- The coach, holding a football, stands 10 yards behind the defensive back (see diagram).
- Other defensive backs should stand adjacent to the drill area.
- The coach passes the football one arm's length from either the left or the right of the defensive back. As the football is in flight, the coach yells "ball" and the defender turns in the designated direction and intercepts or deflects the pass.
- The drill continues until all defensive backs have had a sufficient number of repetitions, turning both left and right.

Coaching Points:

- Instruct the defensive backs to turn the head first and then the rest of the body.
- Insist that defensive backs catch the football in their hands.

Safety Considerations:

- A proper warm-up should precede the drill.
- The drill area should be clear of all foreign articles. This includes the sideline area.
- Helmets should be worn with chinstraps snapped.
- Instruct alternating defensive backs to always remain alert.

Variations:

- Can be used with the football being thrown at varying heights and velocities.
- Can be used with a passer aligned at various distances from the defensive back.
- Can be used with the defensive back turning and sprinting five yards and intercepting or deflecting the pass.
- Can be used as a linebacker or defensive end drill.

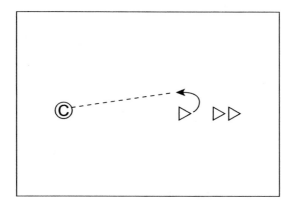

BREAK ON THE BALL DRILL

Phil Elmassian
East Carolina University, University of Minnesota, Virginia Polytechnic Institute, University of Virginia, Syracuse University, University of Washington, Boston College, University of Wisconsin, Louisiana State University, West Virginia University, Marshall University, Purdue University

Objective: To teach and practice the proper fundamentals and techniques of breaking on and intercepting a pass.

Equipment Needed: Line-spacing strip and footballs

Description:

- Place an offensive line-spacing strip on a selected line of scrimmage. A quarterback is aligned in his regular position.
- Position a receiver on each sideline and hash mark 25 yards downfield. Additional receivers are placed five yards downfield and midway between each hash mark and sideline, for a total of six receivers (see diagram).
- A defensive secondary is aligned over a ghost offensive set.
- Alternating defensive backfield units should stand adjacent to the drill area.
- The coach stands behind the defense and directs the quarterback as to his pass drop action and the receiver to whom the pass is to be thrown.
- The coach also directs the defense as to the coverage.
- On the cadence and snap count, the quarterback executes the directed pass drop and passes the football to the designated receiver.
- The defensive unit reacts to the quarterback's pass drop, backpedals to their respective zones, and breaks on and intercepts the thrown pass.
- The defensive back closest to the receiver to whom the pass is thrown is instructed to make the interception as the other defenders position themselves for a possible block.
- The drill continues until all defensive backfields have had a sufficient number of repetitions.
- The drill should be conducted from both left and right alignments and from various field positions.

Coaching Points:

- Always check to see that defensive backs are aligned correctly and are in their proper stances.
- Make sure all defensive backs backpedal correctly.
- Make sure defensive backs accelerate to and intercept each pass at its highest point.
- Instruct defensive backs to return all interceptions down the near sideline.

Safety Considerations:

- A proper warm-up should precede the drill.
- The drill area should be cleared of all foreign articles. This includes the sideline areas.
- Instruct the receivers not to play the football and to avoid all contact with the defensive backs.

Variations:

- Can be used with receivers aligned at varying positions on the field.
- Can be used with the entire secondary.

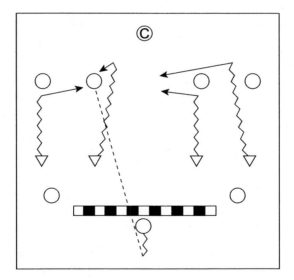

INTERCEPTION DRILL*

Don E. James
Kent State University, University of Washington
National Champions: Washington 1991
National Coach of the Year: Washington 1977 and 1991
College Football Hall of Fame: 1997
AFCA President: 1989

Objective: To teach and practice the proper fundamentals and techniques of breaking on and intercepting the football. Incorporated are skills related to the backpedal, the plant, and the angle to take to a thrown pass.

Equipment Needed: Footballs

Description:

- Position two defensive backs five yards apart at the midpoint of a selected line of scrimmage.
- The coach, holding a football, stands 10 yards in front of the defensive backs. The coach designates a receiver and defender.
- Other defensive backs stand adjacent to the drill area.
- On the coach's signal (shows pass), both defensive backs initiate their backpedal.
- When the defensive backs have backpedaled the desired distance, the coach will turn his shoulders and throw the football to the designated receiver.
- The designated defender reads the coach's shoulder turn and release, and then plants and breaks for the interception.
- The drill continues until all the defensive backs have had a sufficient number of repetitions.

Coaching Points:

- Always check to see that the defensive backs are in their proper stances.
- Insist that the defensive backs execute their backpedal correctly.
- Instruct the defensive backs to get a good plant off their backpedal and to take the proper angle to intercept the football.
- Make sure the defensive backs break in front of the receiver as they intercept the pass at its highest point.

* Reprinted with permission from *101 Winning Football Drills: From the Legends of the Game* by Jerry Tolley

Safety Considerations:

- It is imperative that a proper warm-up precede this drill.
- The defenders should be instructed to drive in front of the receiver and not into him.
- The coach should monitor closely the intensity of the drill.

Variations:

- Can be used with varying distances between the two defensive backs and between the defensive backs and the coach. (The defensive backs can be 10 yards apart and 15 yards from the coach, or the defensive backs can be 15 yards apart and 20 yards from the coach.)
- Can be used with one defensive back positioned five-yards deeper than the other.
- Can be used without designating a receiver.
- Can be used as a linebacker drill.

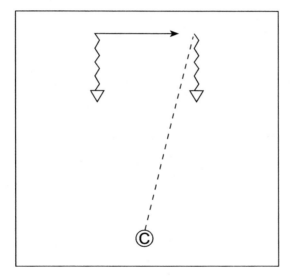

BUILD-UP DRILL (CUSHION-INTERCEPT-WIPE-OUT)

John Calvin Whitehead (Deceased)
Lehigh University
National Champions: 1977
National Coach of the Year: 1977, 1978, 1979

Objective: To teach and practice the proper fundamentals and techniques of covering a receiver and making the interception.

Equipment Needed: Footballs

Description:

- Position a row of receivers perpendicular to a selected line of scrimmage.
- Align a defensive back in his normal position across from the first wide receiver.
- Other defensive backs should stand adjacent to the drill area.
- The quarterback (coach) is positioned in the proper play relationship to the first wide receiver (see diagram).
- On the coach's cadence and snap count, the receiver runs a predetermined pass route and the coach takes a designated pass drop and passes him the football.
- The defensive back *cushions* the receiver and then reacts to and intercepts or deflects the pass.
- The drill continues until all defensive backs have had a sufficient number of repetitions.
- The drill should be conducted to both the left and right and from various positions on the field.

Coaching Points:

- Always check to see that defensive backs are aligned correctly and are in their proper stances.
- Make sure that defensive backs backpedal correctly, keeping their eyes on the passer at all times.
- Instruct defensive backs to get a good plant and to take the proper angle as they react to the receiver's cuts.

Safety Considerations:

- It is imperative that a proper warm-up precedes the drill.
- The drill area should be clear of all foreign articles.
- The drill should progress from form work to live work.
- The coach should closely monitor the intensity of the drill.

Variations:

- Can be used as a wide receiver drill.
- Can be used as a linebacker drill.

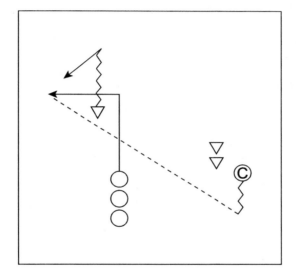

SIDELINE-TACKLING DRILL*

Barry L. Switzer
University of Oklahoma, Dallas Cowboys
National Champions: 1974, 1975, and 1985
Super Bowl XXX Champions
College Football Hall of Fame: 2001

Objective: To teach and practice the proper fundamentals and techniques in executing a sideline tackle.

Equipment Needed: Scrimmage vest (optional) and footballs

Description:

- Position a row of defensive backs on the hash mark and perpendicular to a selected yard line.
- Align a row of ballcarriers 10 yards away from and facing the defensive backs.
- The coach, holding a football, stands in a quarterback pitch relationship to the ballcarriers.
- On command, the coach pitches the football to the first ballcarrier, who runs upfield between the hash marks and sideline.
- The defensive back reads run, initiates his backpedal back and to the outside, and then sprints to an inside-out position on the ballcarrier forcing him to the sideline.
- If the ballcarrier should cut back, the defensive back executes a shoulder tackle. If the ballcarrier continues on his outside path, the defensive back drives him out of bounds.
- The drill continues until all the defensive backs have had a sufficient number of repetitions.
- The drill should be conducted both left and right.

Coaching Points:

- Always check to see that the defensive backs are aligned correctly and are in their proper stances.
- Instruct the tacklers to always maintain an inside-out leverage on the ballcarrier.
- Make sure defensive backs practice proper fundamentals and techniques of safe tackling.

* Reprinted with permission from *101 Winning Football Drills: From the Legends of the Game* by Jerry Tolley

Safety Considerations:

- It is imperative that a proper warm-up precede this drill.
- The drill area should be clear of all foreign articles. This includes the sideline areas.
- The drill should progress from form tackling to live tackling.
- The coach should monitor closely the intensity of the drill.
- The coach should watch for and eliminate all unacceptable matchups as to size and athletic ability.
- Instruct all defensive backs in the proper fundamentals and techniques of safe tackling.
- The training staff should be placed on special alert.

Variations:

- Can be used as a form or live tackling drill.
- Can be used as an offensive back drill.
- Can be used as a defensive end and linebacker drill.

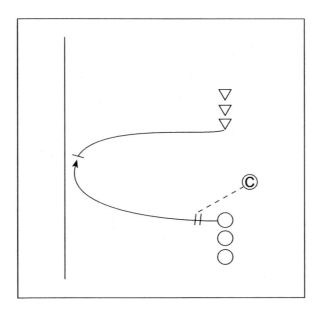

RABBIT TACKLING

Robert J. "Bob" Thalman
Hampton-Sydney College, University of North Carolina,
Georgia Institute of Technology, Virginia Military Institute

Objective: To teach and practice the proper fundamentals and techniques of open-field tackling.

Equipment Needed: Four cones and footballs

Description:

- Align a ballcarrier, holding a football, midway between the right hash mark and the near sideline on the plus 25 yard line.

- A defensive back is positioned in front of the ballcarrier on the 10 yard line. Another defender (the *rabbit*) is placed five yards behind the ballcarrier.

- Other defensive backs should stand adjacent to the drill area and yell encouragement to their teammates.

- The boundaries of the drill are formed by the hash marks, the sideline, the 25 yard line, and the goal line (see diagram).

- On the coach's command, the ballcarrier sprints for the goal line as the front-facing defensive back executes the open-field tackle.

- The ballcarrier is instructed to cut either left or right to avoid the tackle. The *rabbit* is instructed to chase the ballcarrier to ensure that he does not hesitate too long as he tries to avoid the defender. (The *rabbit* is not allowed to tackle the ballcarrier but he can tag him.)

- The drill continues until all defensive backs have had a sufficient number of repetitions.

- The drill also should be conducted from the left hash mark.

Coaching Points:

- Always check to see that defensive backs are in their proper stances.

- Instruct the defensive backs to force the ballcarrier to an angle tackling position.

- Instruct the defensive backs to always focus on the hip area of the ballcarrier.

- Instruct the defensive backs in the proper fundamentals and techniques of safe tackling.

Safety Considerations:

- It is imperative that proper a warm-up precedes the drill.
- The drill area should be clear of all foreign articles. This includes the sideline areas.
- The drill should progress from form tackling to live tackling.
- The coach should closely monitor the intensity of the drill.
- The coach should watch for and eliminate all unacceptable match-ups of size and athletic ability.
- Instruct the *rabbit* that he is never to tackle the ballcarrier.
- Instruct the ballcarrier that he is never to run straight over the defensive back.
- Make sure all defensive backs practice proper fundamentals and techniques of safe tackling.
- The training staff should be placed on special alert.

Variations:

- Can be used as a form or live-tackling drill.
- Can be used without the *rabbit*.
- Can be used as a running back drill.
- Can be used as a defensive end or linebacker drill.

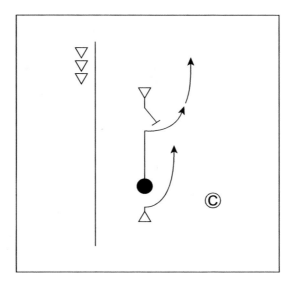

TACKLE-AND-PURSUIT DRILL*

George T. Welsh
United States Naval Academy, University of Virginia
National Coach of the Year: Virginia 1989, 1991, and 1998
College Football Hall of Fame: 2004

Objective: To teach and practice the proper fundamentals and techniques of pursuit and sideline tackling.

Equipment Needed: Six cones and footballs

Description:

- Align two rows of ballcarriers three-yards apart and perpendicular to a selected line of scrimmage. The first two ballcarriers hold footballs.

- Place three cones to form a 15-yard equilateral triangle on each side of the two rows of ballcarriers. The base of the triangle is placed on the selected line of scrimmage. The bases of the two triangles are also 15 yards apart (see diagram).

- Position a row of defensive backs two yards off the line of scrimmage and facing the two rows of ballcarriers.

- The coach stands behind the defensive backs and signals one ballcarrier to run straight ahead, and the other to circle behind the apex of the triangle and to proceed upfield.

- On the coach's command, the designated ballcarrier runs straight ahead and the defensive back reacts and executes a form tackle. The tackler holds the form tackle until the coach blows his whistle.

- When the coach blows his whistle, the tackler releases the first ballcarrier and pursues and form tackles the second ballcarrier who is running at a controlled pace around the triangle.

- The drill continues until all the defensive backs have had a sufficient number of repetitions both left and right.

Coaching Points:

- Always check to see that the defensive backs are in their proper stances.

- Instruct the defensive backs to maintain the first tackle until they hear the coach's whistle.

- Make sure the defensive backs take the proper pursuit angle as they move to make the second tackle.

* Reprinted with permission from *101 Winning Football Drills: From the Legends of the Game* by Jerry Tolley

- The coach should move with the defenders and watch both of their tackles.
- Make sure the defensive backs practice proper fundamentals and techniques of safe tackling.

Safety Considerations:

- It is imperative that a proper warm-up precede this drill.
- The drill area should be clear of all foreign articles.
- The drill should progress from half speed to full speed (not live).
- The coach should monitor closely the intensity of the drill.
- The coach should watch for and eliminate all unacceptable match-ups as to size and athletic ability.
- Instruct all defensive backs in proper fundamentals and techniques of safe tackling.

Variation:

- Can be used by all defensive positions.

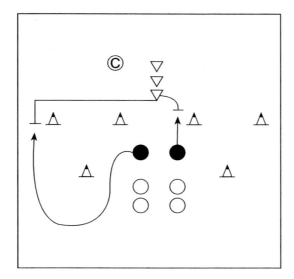

RUN-PASS REACTION DRILL

Fredrick H. "Fred" Dunlap
University of Buffalo, Cornell University, Lehigh University, Colgate University

Objective: To teach and practice the proper fundamentals and techniques in executing the backpedal and reacting to a run or pass. Skills related to intercepting a pass are also incorporated.

Equipment Needed: Footballs

Description:

- Align a defensive back in the *football position* on a selected yard line.
- The coach, holding a football, is positioned five yards in front of the defensive back.
- Other defensive backs should stand adjacent to the drill area.
- On the coach's signal (ball slap), the defensive back initiates his backpedal.
- The coach executes one of two maneuvers. He can either tuck the football under his arm, indicating run, or he can raise the football over his head, indicating a pass.
- The defensive back reads the coach's signal. If it is a running play, he sprints to and breaks down one yard in front of the coach. If the coach signals a pass, the defensive back continues his backpedal and awaits the coach's pass.
- When pass is signaled, the coach waits for the defensive back to backpedal 8 to 12 yards and then throws the pass either to his left or right.
- The defensive back breaks on the thrown football, makes the interception, and sprints upfield and past the coach.
- The drill continues until all defensive backs have had a sufficient number of repetitions.

Coaching Points:

- Always check to see that defensive backs are in their proper stances.
- Insist that defensive backs backpedal correctly.
- Instruct the defensive backs to always watch the quarterback (coach) and to yell run on run plays, pass on pass plays, ball when the pass is thrown, and *bingo* when the interception is made.
- Make sure defensive backs intercept all passes at their highest point.

Safety Considerations:

- A proper warm-up should precede the drill.
- The drill area should be clear of all foreign articles.

Variation:

- Can be used as a linebacker drill.

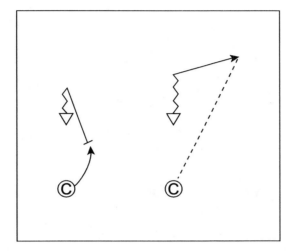

TECHNIQUE-AND-AGILITY DRILL*

> ## Hugh "Duffy" Daugherty (Deceased)
> Michigan State University
> National Champions: 1955, 1957, 1965, and 1966
> National Coach of the Year: 1955 and 1965
> College Football Hall of Fame: 1984
> Amos Alonzo Stagg Award: 1985

Objective: To develop general agility, reaction, quickness, body control, and peripheral vision.

Equipment Needed: Four cones and a stopwatch

Description:

- Place four cones 20 yards apart to form a square.
- Position a row of defensive backs outside the cone at the right front of the square (see diagram).
- The coach also stands at the front of the square.
- On the coach's command, the first defensive back assumes a good football position and then executes a *carioca* across the front of the drill area. He then runs backward to the second cone, *cariocas* to the third, and then sprints past the last cone. The defensive back is instructed to face the coach throughout the drill.
- The drill progresses from half speed to full speed.
- The drill continues until all the defensive backs have had a sufficient number of repetitions.

Coaching Points:

- Make sure the defensive backs execute the *cariocas* correctly.
- Insist that the defensive backs maintain the desired body position as they make their backward run.
- Make sure the defensive backs sprint past the last cone.
- Instruct the defensive backs to always face the front of the drill area throughout the drill.

---

* Reprinted with permission from *101 Winning Football Drills: From the Legends of the Game* by Jerry Tolley

Safety Considerations:

- Proper warm-up should precede the drill.
- Players with knee problems should be excused from this drill.
- Maintain a minimum distance of 15 yards between performing drill participants.

Variations:

- Can be used as a motivation drill by timing defensive backs once a week.
- Can be used as a general agility drill.

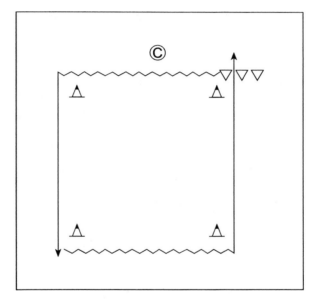

SIDELINE TACKLING DRILL

Bob S. Haley
California University of Pennsylvania, Shepherd College

Objective: To teach and practice the proper fundamentals and techniques in executing a sideline tackle. Skills related to agility, reaction, and quickness are also incorporated.

Equipment Needed: One cone and footballs

Description:

- Position a cone seven to eight yards from the sideline on a selected line of scrimmage.
- Align a ballcarrier 1.5 yards in front of the cone (see diagram).
- A defensive back lines up three yards in front of the ballcarrier.
- The coach, holding a football, is positioned between the defensive back and the ballcarrier.
- Other drill participants should stand adjacent to drill area.
- On command, the coach pitches the football to the ballcarrier, who circles the cones, squares up, and runs down the sideline.
- Also on the coach's command, the defensive back initiates his backpedal, reads run, and executes the sideline tackle while maintaining an inside-out leverage on the ballcarrier.
- The drill continues until all defensive backs have had a sufficient number of repetitions.
- The drill should be conducted to both the left and right.

Coaching Points:

- Always check to see that defensive backs are in their proper stances.
- Make sure that defensive backs backpedal correctly.
- Instruct the defensive backs to keep their shoulders square to the line of scrimmage and to maintain an inside-out relationship to the ballcarrier.
- Make sure defensive backs practice the proper fundamentals and techniques of safe tackling.

Safety Considerations:

- It is imperative that a proper warm-up precedes the drill.
- The drill area should be clear of all foreign articles. This includes the sideline area.
- The drill should progress from form tackling to live tackling.
- The coach should closely monitor the intensity of the drill.
- The coach should watch for and eliminate all unacceptable match-ups of size and athletic ability.
- Instruct all defensive backs in proper fundamentals and techniques of safe tackling.
- The training staff should be placed on special alert.

Variations:

- Can be used as a form tackling or live tackling drill.
- Can be used as a defensive end or linebacker drill.

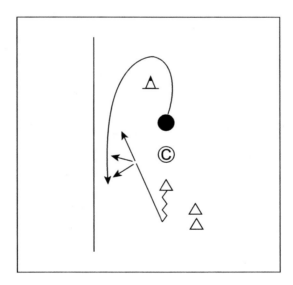

STEM AND BREAK*

Robert "Bobby" Wallace
University of North Alabama, Temple University
National Champions: North Alabama 1993, 1994, and 1995
National Coach of the Year: North Alabama 1993, 1994, and 1995

Objective: To teach and practice the proper fundamentals and techniques of maintaining vertical and horizontal leverage on a receiver when in man-to-man coverage.

Equipment Needed: Four cones and a football

Description:

- Place four cones one yard apart on a selected line of scrimmage.
- Align a defensive back five yards behind and facing the cone on his far right. (See diagram)
- The coach holding a football is positioned on the opposite side of the cones and facing the defensive back. The coach remains stationary throughout the drill.
- Other defensive backs stand adjacent to the drill area.
- On the coach's cadence and snap count, the defensive back begins his backpedal.
- At a point during the backpedal determined by the coach, the coach moves the football laterally pointing in the direction of the second cone. The defensive back reacts to the coach's ball movements and *stems* back at a 45-degree angle to the second cone.
- When the defensive back is positioned behind the second cone he once again goes into his backpedal and looks for and reacts to the coach's lateral-ball movement by *stemming* to the third cone.
- After the defensive back has *stemmed* from the backpedal in front of cone three, he plants his outside foot and breaks back upfield at a 45-degree angle catching the pass thrown by the coach.
- The drill continues until all the defensive backs have had a sufficient number of repetitions moving both to the left and the right.

* Reprinted with permission from *101 Winning Football Drills: From the Legends of the Game* by Jerry Tolley

Coaching Points:

- Always check to see that the defensive backs are in their proper stances.
- Instruct the defensive backs to execute the backpedal correctly by keeping their shoulders squared to the line of scrimmage.
- Instruct the defensive backs to execute the *stem* correctly by keeping their shoulders squared to the line of scrimmage as they gain width and depth while stepping laterally. (No crossover stepping is permitted.)
- Instruct the defensive backs to watch the coach and his ball movement at all times when moving to catch the thrown pass.
- Insist that the defensive backs drive off their back foot, catch the ball at its highest point, and yell oskie as they sprint for the touchdown.

Safety Considerations:

- Proper warm-up should precede the drill.
- The drill area should be clear of all foreign articles.

Variation:

- Can be used as a linebacker drill.

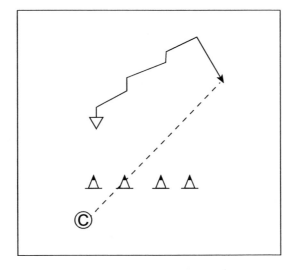

TACKLING DRILL

Richard "Rick" Solomon
Dubuque University, Southern Illinois University, University of Iowa,
Syracuse University, University of Illinois, New York Giants,
Minnesota Vikings, Western Illinois State University, Arizona Cardinals

Objective: To teach and practice the proper fundamentals and techniques of safe tackling.

Equipment Needed: None

Description:

- Align defensive backs five yards apart on a selected yard line.
- Align ballcarriers in a corresponding position five yards in front of and facing the defensive backs.
- On the coach's command the ballcarriers begin walking at a 45-degree angle to a designated side of the defensive backs (see diagram).
- The defensive backs react and execute form tackles on the ballcarriers.
- The drill progresses from walk-through to full speed (not live).
- The drill continues until all defensive backs have had a sufficient number of repetitions to both the left and right.

Coaching Points:

- Always check to see that defensive backs are in a good *football position*.
- Make sure defensive backs execute all tackles on the rise and with their heads up.
- Insist that defensive backs select an aiming point through the outside number of the ballcarrier.
- Instruct the defensive backs to follow through and to wrap up the ballcarrier.
- Make sure defensive backs practice the proper fundamentals and techniques of safe tackling.

Safety Considerations:

- It is imperative that a proper warm-up precedes the drill.
- The drill area should be clear of all foreign articles.
- A minimum distance of five yards should be maintained between each pair of drill participants.
- The drill should progress from walk-through to full speed (not live).
- The coach should closely monitor the intensity of the drill.
- The coach should watch for and eliminate all unacceptable match-ups of size and athletic ability.
- Instruct all defensive backs in the proper fundamentals and techniques of safe tackling.

Variation:

- Can be used for all defensive positions.

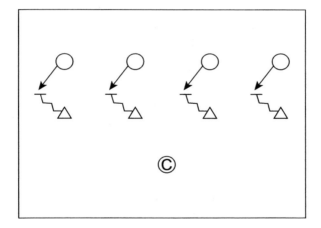

THREE LINE STRETCH DRILL

Bobby C. Pate
Western Carolina University, West Georgia College
National Champions: West Georgia College 1982
National Coach of the Year: West Georgia College 1982

Objective: To teach and practice the proper fundamentals and techniques of the backpedal and breaking on and intercepting a pass.

Equipment Needed: Footballs

Description:

- Position two rows of receivers 10 yards apart and perpendicular to the sideline, facing the field (see diagram).
- The coach, holding a football, stands on the sideline midway between the two lines of receivers.
- A defensive back is positioned 9 to 11 yards in front of and facing the coach.
- Other defensive backs should stand adjacent to the drill area.
- On the cadence and snap count, the coach executes a five-step pass drop as the first receiver in each line runs a *streak* pattern down his yard line at three-quarter speed. The defensive back reacts and initiates his backpedal.
- The coach now makes a definite head and shoulder turn and passes the football to either of the receivers, and the defensive back sprints to the football and makes the interception. He then yells *bingo* and sprints past the coach, handing him the football.
- The drill continues until all defensive backs have had a sufficient number of repetitions to both the left and right.

Coaching Points:

- Always check to see that defensive backs are aligned correctly and are in their proper stances.
- Insist that defensive backs backpedal correctly.
- Instruct the defensive backs to always watch the quarterback's (coach's) eyes first and then his shoulder turn.
- Make sure the defensive backs intercept the football at its highest point.

Safety Considerations:

- A proper warm-up should precede the drill.
- The drill area should be clear of all foreign articles. This includes the sideline area.
- Instruct receivers to avoid all contact with defensive backs.
- Instruct returning receivers to stay clear of the drill area.

Variations:

- Can be used with receivers running full speed.
- Can be used with the coach throwing the football at varying distances, trajectories, and speeds.
- Can be used as a conditioning drill.

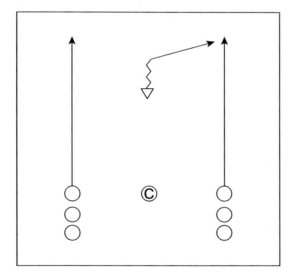

THROUGH THE BALL DRILL

Danny L. Ford
University of Alabama, Virginia Polytechnic Institute,
Clemson University, University of Arkansas
National Champions: Clemson 1981
National Coach of the Year: Clemson 1981

Objective: To teach and practice the proper fundamentals and techniques of breaking through a receiver to intercept a pass or to break on and intercept a tipped pass.

Equipment Needed: One large blocking dummy and footballs

Description:

- Align a quarterback (coach), holding a football, on a selected line of scrimmage.
- Place a blocking dummy in a curl pattern relationship to the quarterback.
- Position a defensive back in his normal alignment to the curl area.
- Other defensive backs should stand adjacent to the drill area.
- A manager, holding a football, stands adjacent to the curl area.
- On cadence, the coach initiates his pass drop as the defensive back executes his backpedal.
- The coach either passes the football in the direction of the dummy or to the manager, who tips it into the air.
- The defensive back reads the coach's pass, and if the football is thrown in the curl area, he breaks through the dummy and makes the interception. If the football is thrown to the manager, the defensive back breaks off the curl pattern and intercepts the *tipped* pass.

Coaching Points:

- Always check to see that defensive backs are aligned correctly and are in their proper stances.
- Insist that defensive backs backpedal correctly.
- Instruct defensive backs to initiate their breaks on the coach's motion and not wait until the football is in the air.
- Make sure that the defensive backs intercept the football at its highest point.

Safety Considerations:

- A proper warm-up should precede the drill.
- The drill area should be clear of all foreign articles.
- Instruct the manager to *tip* the football well clear of himself.

Variations:

- Can be used with the dummy placed at various pass pattern completion points (post, hook, flag, etc.).
- Can be used with managers standing at various positions adjacent to the dummy.

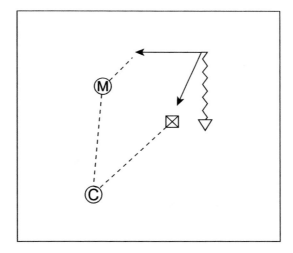

TOWEL DRILL

Frank R. Burns
John Hopkins University, Rutgers University
National Coach of the Year: Rutgers University 1976

Objective: To teach and practice the proper fundamentals and techniques of breaking on and intercepting a thrown football from a one-third deep alignment.

Equipment Needed: Three towels and footballs

Description:

- Position a quarterback (coach) holding a football at the midpoint of a selected line of scrimmage.
- A towel is placed directly in front of the coach 15 yards downfield. Additional towels are placed three yards outside the hash marks 20 yards downfield.
- A defensive back lines up, facing the coach, one yard behind the middle towel (see diagram).
- Other defensive backs line up in a straight line 15 yards directly behind the first defensive back.
- On the cadence and snap count, the coach executes a four-step pass drop and passes the football in the direction of one of the three towels.
- The defensive back reads the quarterback and initiates his backpedal. Then, on the quarterback's long arm motion, he breaks on and intercepts the football at its highest point.
- When the pass is intercepted, the defender yells *bingo* and sprints to and hands the football to the coach.
- The drill continues until all participants have had a sufficient number of repetitions.

Coaching Points:

- Always check to see that defensive backs are aligned correctly and are in their proper stances.
- Insist that defensive backs backpedal correctly.
- Instruct defensive backs to watch the quarterback (coach) and to get a good plant as they sprint directly to the designated towel. Once the football is thrown, the defensive backs focus their eyes on the towel and close the distance to the football. They again pick up the flight of the pass when they are four yards from the towel.
- Make sure that the defensive backs intercept the football at its highest point.

Safety Considerations:

- A proper warm-up should precede the drill.
- The drill area should be clear of all foreign articles.

Variations:

- Can be used to teach and practice the proper fundamentals and techniques of breaking on and intercepting a football from a one-half deep alignment. (Towels are placed two yards from the sideline 15 yards downfield and at midfield 20 yards downfield. Defensive backs straddle the hash marks 12 yards downfield from the middle towel.)
- Can be used with crash mats instead of towels and have defensive backs dive for the interceptions.
- Can be used with a variety of quarterback pass drops.

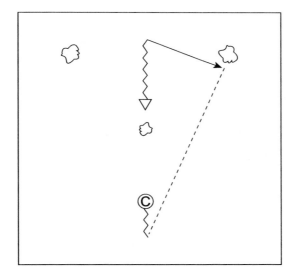

ZONE LEVERAGE DRILL

Ed Buffum
Kansas State Teachers College, University of Iowa, University of Wisconsin, Southwestern Oklahoma State University

Objective: To teach and practice the proper fundamentals and techniques of breaking on and intercepting a pass.

Equipment Needed: Footballs

Description:

- Position a coach, holding a football, at the midpoint of a selected line of scrimmage.
- Align a row of receivers perpendicular to the line of scrimmage and five yards from a sideline.
- A defensive back is positioned eight yards downfield and in front of and facing the coach (see diagram).
- Other defensive backs stand adjacent to the drill area.
- On the cadence and snap count, the coach executes a straight dropback pass drop and passes the football to the first receiver, who is sprinting down the field.
- The defensive back reads the coach's pass drop and executes his backpedal. On the coach's shoulder turn, he breaks on and intercepts the pass at its highest point.
- The defensive back then sprints down the sideline and returns the football to the coach.
- The drill continues until all defensive backs have had a sufficient number of repetitions.
- The drill should be conducted to both the left and right.

Coaching Points:

- Always check to see that the defensive backs are in their proper stances.
- Insist that defensive backs stay in and execute their backpedals correctly until the coach turns his shoulders to pass the football.
- Instruct the defensive backs to look directly at the coach and also to keep the receiver in their field of vision. If the receiver should outrun the defensive back's field of vision, the defensive back then turns and runs with the receiver to regain the lost ground.
- Make sure the defensive backs break in front of the receiver and intercept the pass at its highest point.

Safety Considerations:

- A proper warm-up should precede the drill.
- The drill area should be clear of all foreign articles. This includes the sideline areas.
- Instruct the receivers to avoid all contact with the defensive backs.
- Make sure returning pass receivers stay well clear of the drill area.

Variations:

- Can be used with the coach passing the football from various positions between the hash marks.
- Can be used with receivers running down both sidelines at the same time.

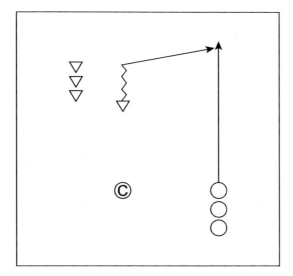

BACKPEDAL PROGRAM*

Vincent J. "Vince" Dooley
University of Georgia
National Champions: 1980
National Coach of the Year: 1980 and 1982
College Football Hall of Fame: 1994
Amos Alonzo Stagg Award: 2001
AFCA President: 1985

Objective: To teach and practice the proper fundamentals in executing the backpedal. Incorporated are skills related to agility, reaction, and acceleration.

Equipment Needed: Football

Description:

- Align two defensive backs 10 yards apart across from a selected line of scrimmage.
- The coach, holding a football, is positioned in between the defenders on the line of scrimmage.
- Other defensive backs stand adjacent to the drill area.
- The drill is conducted in seven phases as follows:
  - *Back and forth.* On the coach's command, the defensive backs drive from their stances and backpedal for five yards and then push forward for five yards. Procedure is repeated ten times (see diagram A).
  - *Backpedal: come straight back to front.* On the coach's command, the defensive backs drive from their stances and backpedal for 10 yards and then push off the back foot and sprint back to their original positions. Procedure is repeated five or six times, alternating pushing off the left and right foot (see diagram B).
  - *Backpedal: push right or left.* On the coach's command, the defensive backs drive from their stances and backpedal for 10 yards and then cut and sprint 10 yards at a 90-degree angle. Procedure is repeated five times with the defensive backs sprinting both left and right (see diagram C).
  - *Backpedal: push up and in at a 45-degree angle.* On the coach's command, the defensive backs drive from their stances and backpedal for 10 yards and then cut and sprint 10 yards at 45-degree angles toward the line of scrimmage. Procedure is repeated five times with the defensive backs sprinting at 45-degree angles both left and right (see diagram D).

- *Backpedal: turn and break deep at a 45-degree angle.* On the coach's command, the defensive backs drive from their stances and backpedal for 10 yards and then cut and sprint 10 yards at 45-degree angles away from the line of scrimmage. Procedure is repeated five times with the defensive backs sprinting at 45-degree angles both left and right (see diagram E).

- *Backpedal: turn deep at a 45-degree angle; roll around on deep throw back.* On the coach's command, the preceding procedure is repeated. However, after the ten-yard 45-degree angle sprint away from the line of scrimmage, the defensive backs turn completely around with their backs away from the line of scrimmage and sprint back at 45-degree angles. Procedure is repeated five times with the defensive backs turning and sprinting both left and right (see diagram F).

- *Backpedal for speed.* On the coach's command, the defensive backs backpedal for speed at distances of 10 yards, 20 yards, and 40 yards. Procedure is repeated five times at each distance.

Coaching Points:

- Always check to see that the defensive backs are in their proper stances.
- Instruct the defensive backs to keep a base of six to eight inches with their toes pointing straight ahead as they execute all backpedals.
- Insist that the defensive backs maintain a low center of gravity with the weight on the front foot. Heels should never touch the ground.
- Make sure the defensive backs keep their head up throughout the drill.
- Emphasize that all breaks off the backpedals should coincide with a particular pass pattern to be covered (out, curl, flag, post, etc.).
- Insist that the drill be conducted at full speed.

Safety Considerations:

- A proper warm-up should precede the drill with particular emphasis on the lower back, hamstrings, and groin.
- The drill area should be clear of all foreign articles.
- Maintain a minimum distance of 10 yards between performing drill participants.

Variation:

- Can be used with the coach executing a pass drop and throwing passes.

A

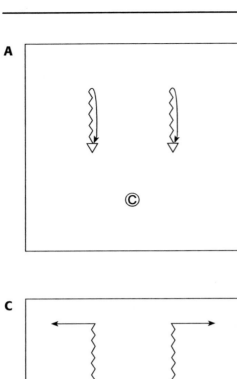

B

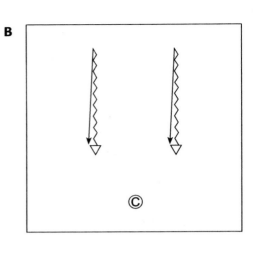

C

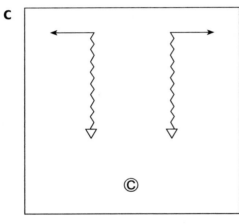

D

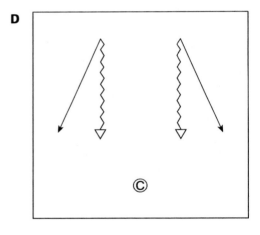

E

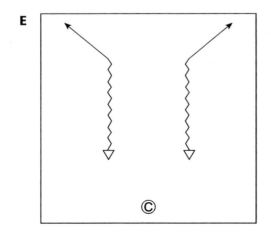

F

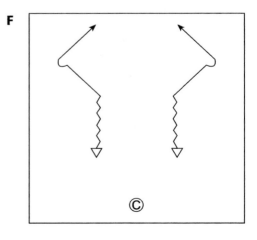

BACKWARD RUNNING DRILL

> **Jack A. Harbaugh**
> Morehead State University, Bowling Green State University,
> University of Iowa, University of Michigan, Samford University,
> Western Michigan University, University of Pittsburgh, Western Michigan University
> National Champions: Western Kentucky 2002
> National Coach of the Year: Western Kentucky 2002

Objective: To teach and practice the proper fundamentals and techniques in executing the backpedal.

Equipment Needed: Footballs

Description:

- Align a defensive back facing the sideline at the junction of a selected yard line and the sideline.
- The coach, holding a football, is positioned off the field and two yards in front of the defender.
- Other defensive backs should stand adjacent to drill area.
- The drill is conducted in four phases, as follows:
  - Back and sprint. On the coach's signal, the defensive back backpedals down the yard line to the hash mark. When the defender reaches the hash mark, the coach gives a second signal indicating that a pass has been thrown deep. (No pass is actually thrown.) The defensive back reacts to the second signal and turns and sprints straight down the yard line. It is important that the defender keep his eyes on the coach as he turns and sprints.

  - Back and 45-degrees up. On the coach's signal, the defensive back backpedals down the yard line. When the defender has reached the desired depth, the coach gives a second signal and the defensive back reacts and breaks at a 45-degree angle toward the sideline. The coach then passes the football and the defender makes the interception and sprints across the sideline.

  - Back and 45-degrees back. On the coach's signal, the defensive back backpedals down the yard line. When the defender has reached the desired depth, the coach gives a second signal and the defensive back reacts and breaks at a 45-degree angle away from the sideline. The coach then passes the football and the defender makes the interception and sprints across the sideline.

– Back and over the wrong shoulder. Same as the preceding phase except that after the 45-degree break away from the sideline, the coach passes the football over the defender's wrong shoulder. This forces the defender to turn his back away from the coach as he breaks to intercept the football and sprints across the sideline.

- The drill continues until all defensive backs have had a sufficient number of repetitions.
- All breaks should be conducted to both the left and right.

Coaching Points:

- Always check to see that that the defensive backs are in their proper stances.
- Instruct defensive backs to stay low and on the balls of their feet with their arms pumping as they execute their backpedal.
- Insist that the defensive backs keep their eyes on the passer throughout all phases of the drill.
- Emphasize that all breaks off the backpedal coincide with a particular pass pattern to be covered (long ball over shoulder, out, post, flag, over wrong shoulder, etc.).
- Insist that the drill be conducted at full speed.

Safety Considerations:

- A proper warm-up should precede the drill.
- The drill area should be clear of all foreign articles. This includes the sideline area.

Variations:

- Can be used with two or more defensive backs at the same time.
- Can be used as a linebacker drill.

A

B

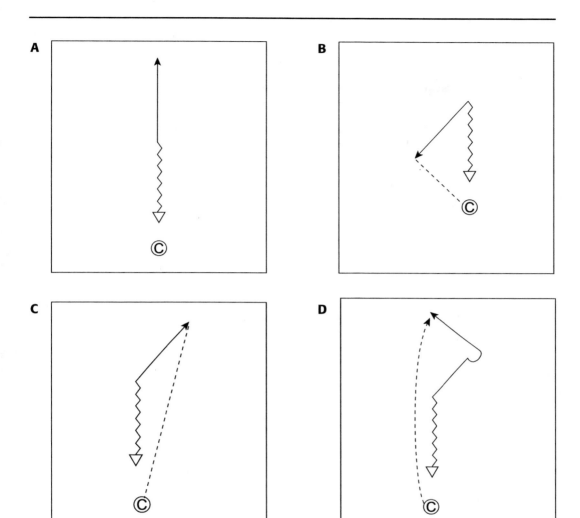

C

D

5

Tackling Drills

LEVERAGE TACKLE

Lloyd H. Carr
Eastern Michigan University, University of Illinois, University of Michigan
National Champions: Michigan 1997
National Coach of the Year: Michigan 1997

Objective: To teach and practice the proper fundamentals and techniques of coming to balance from a full-speed pursuit in the execution of a tackle.

Equipment Needed: Two pop-up dummies and a football

Description:

- Position a ballcarrier splitting the uprights on a selected goal line.
- Position two tacklers in *football positions* 30 yards downfield, each aligned with a goalpost.
- Place two pop-up dummies on the 25 yard line, each aligned with a goalpost upright (see diagram).
- Other drill participants should stand adjacent to the drill area.
- The coach also stands adjacent to the drill area.
- On the coach's command, the tacklers attack the onside pop-up dummy (simulated blocker), avoiding the block while maintaining their alignment on their goalpost upright.
- Once the tacklers clear the dummy area, the ballcarrier runs upfield. (In running up the field, the ballcarrier's only restriction is that his running path must remain between the hash marks).
- The tacklers, working in unison, react to the movement of the ballcarrier, and after maintaining the initial separation, *come to balance*, regain the *football position*, and close on and *thud-up* the ballcarrier.
- The drill continues until all tacklers have had a sufficient number of repetitions from both the left and right side of the field.

Coaching Points:

- Always check to see that tacklers begin the drill in the *football-ready* position.
- Instruct the tacklers to run full-speed and to hit the pop-up dummy with a quick avoidance move.
- Make sure tacklers maintain proper separation (never follow the same color jersey downfield) until they converge on the ballcarrier.

- Instruct the tacklers to always keep the ballcarrier in front and to the inside, forcing him back in the direction of the converging teammate.
- When *coming to balance*, instruct the tacklers to bend their knees, *buzz* their feet, keep their shoulders squared, and keep their eyes up, focusing on the ballcarrier.
- Instruct all tacklers to avoid crossover stepping, lunging, and ducking the head.

Safety Considerations:

- A proper warm-up should precede the drill.
- The drill area should be clear of all foreign articles.
- The ballcarrier should always pull up on contact and never attempt to run through the tacklers.
- Full equipment should be worn.

Variation:

- Can be used as a no-pads and helmet-only drill (when used with no pads, the tacklers are instructed not to *thud-up*, but only to *tag-off* the ballcarrier).

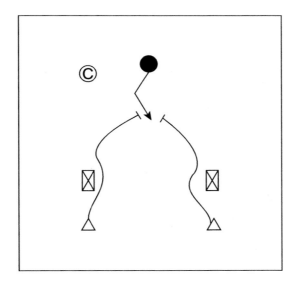

TERRAPIN TACKLING DRILL

> ## Ralph H. Friedgen
> The Citadel, The College of William and Mary, Murray State University,
> San Diego Chargers, Georgia Institute of Technology, University of Maryland
> National Assistant Coach of the Year: Georgia Tech 1999
> National Coach of the Year: Maryland 2001

Objective: To teach and practice the proper fundamentals and techniques of executing an angle tackle.

Equipment Needed: Footballs and four cones

Description:

- Place four cones five yards apart to form a square.
- Position a tackler midway between the front two cones.
- Position a ballcarrier in a front-facing alignment to the tackler midway between the opposite two cones (see diagram).
- Other drill participants should stand adjacent to the drill area.
- The coach is positioned to the right or left of the tackler.
- On the coach's command, the ballcarrier initiates his running path at a 45-degree angle to either the left or right.
- The tackler reacts to the run of the ballcarrier and executes the tackle.
- The drill continues until all participants have had a sufficient number of repetitions.

Coaching Points:

- Always check to see that tacklers begin the drill in a good *football position*.
- Instruct tacklers to always approach the ballcarrier from an inside-out relationship using the sideline as a *twelfth defender*.
- Emphasize the importance of executing the tackle on the rise, wrapping the arms, and accelerating the feet through the ballcarrier.
- Make sure all tacklers practice the proper fundamentals and techniques of

safe tackling.

Safety Considerations:

- A proper warm-up should precede the drill.
- The drill area should be clear of all foreign articles.
- The drill should progress from form tackling to full-speed tackling.
- Instruct all tacklers in the proper fundamentals and techniques of safe tackling.
- The coach should closely monitor the intensity of the drill.
- The coach should watch for and eliminate all unacceptable match-ups as to size and athletic ability.
- Instruct the tacklers to never take the ballcarrier to the ground.

Variations:

- When used with young and inexperienced players, the drill area can be reduced in size.
- Can be used as a running back drill.

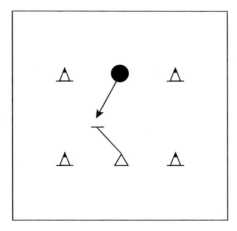

FACE DRILL*

Ara Raoul Parseghian
Miami University (OH), Northwestern University, University of Notre Dame
National Champions: Notre Dame 1964, 1966, and 1973
National Coach of the Year: Notre Dame 1964
College Football Hall of Fame: 1980
Amos Alonzo Stagg Award: 1997

Objective: To teach and practice the proper fundamentals and techniques of open-field tackling. Incorporated are skills related to running, agility, reaction, and quickness.

Equipment Needed: Three large blocking dummies

Description:

- Position three held dummies five yards apart on a selected line of scrimmage. The coach holds the middle dummy.
- Align a row of tacklers 20 yards downfield, facing the middle dummy.
- On the coach's command, the first tackler sprints straight for the middle dummy.
- As he approaches the dummy area, the coach signals the tackler to move either left or right by tilting his dummy.
- The tackler reacts and executes the tackle on the dummy to the designated side.
- The drill continues until all the drill participants have had a sufficient number of tackles.

Coaching Points:

- Make sure that all the drill participants square up to the dummy before executing the tackle.
- Emphasize the importance of wrapping the arms on all tackles.
- Make sure that all personnel practice the proper fundamentals and techniques of safe tackling.
- Insist that the drill be conducted at full speed.

* Reprinted with permission from *101 Winning Football Drills: From the Legends of the Game* by Jerry Tolley

Safety Considerations:

- A proper warm-up should precede the drill.
- The drill area should be clear of all foreign articles.
- Instruct all the personnel in the proper fundamentals and techniques of safe tackling.
- Dummy holders should be instructed to release dummies as each tackle is being executed.

Variations:

- Can vary the distance at which tacklers line up from dummy area.
- Can vary the distance between dummies.
- Coach can signal tacklers at various times, or delay signal and instruct tacklers to break down working their feet, before tilting the dummy.

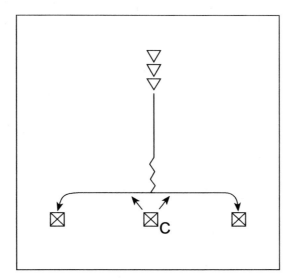

HIT AND LIFT

Ron Turner
University of Arizona, Northwestern University, University of Pittsburgh,
University of Southern California, Texas A&M University, Stanford University,
San Jose State University, Chicago Bears, University of Illinois

Objective: To introduce, teach, and practice the proper fundamentals and techniques of tackling.

Equipment Needed: None

Description:

- Align a row of ballcarriers five yards apart on a selected line of scrimmage.
- Align a row of tacklers four yards in front of and facing the ballcarriers (see diagram).
- The coach stands adjacent to the drill participants and views the hit and lift tackle from various angles, particularly from behind the ballcarriers.
- On the coach's command the first tackler drives from the *football position* and executes the hit and lift tackle on the ballcarrier.
- The ballcarrier stays in his stationary *football ready* position and jumps slightly just before the tackler executes the *hit and lift* tackle.
- The drill can be conducted with tacklers executing the *hit and lift* tackles one at a time or in unison.
- The drill continues until all tacklers have had a sufficient number of repetitions.

Coaching Points:

- Always check to see that tacklers are in their proper *football ready* position.
- Instruct all tacklers to focus their eyes on the contact point, which is the area from the top of the numbers to the pads.
- Instruct the tacklers to *shoot the hands* forward with eyes focused to the sky as contact is made.
- Insist that the tacklers execute the tackle keeping the back flat, the head up, and hands above the elbows, wrapping the arms and *grabbing cloth*.
- Emphasize the importance of driving the feet through the ballcarrier on all tackles.
- Make sure tacklers practice the proper fundamentals and techniques of safe tackling.

Safety Considerations:

- A proper warm-up should precede the drill.
- The drill area should be clear of all foreign articles.
- This drill should not be conducted as a full-speed or live tackling drill.
- The coach should watch for and eliminate all unacceptable match-ups as to size and athletic ability.
- Instruct all tacklers in the proper fundamentals and techniques of safe tackling.

Variations:

- Can be used as an angle tackling drill with the ballcarrier turned at a 45-degree angle.
- Can be used with the tacklers shedding a block before executing the tackle.
- Can have the tacklers *skate* before executing the tackle.

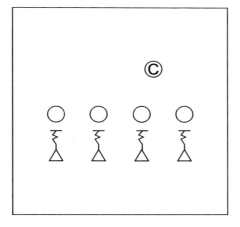

ANGLE TACKLING

Jim Boccher

Central Michigan, Rutgers University, Ferris State University, University of Michigan

Objective: To teach and practice the proper fundamentals and techniques of tackling.

Equipment Needed: Three cones and a football

Description:

- Form a triangle by placing two cones six yards apart on a selected line of scrimmage and a third cone four yards in front and midway between the other two cones (see diagram).
- Position a ballcarrier straddling the cone at the apex of the triangle.
- A tackler is positioned midway between the two cones that form the base of the triangle.
- Other drill participants should stand adjacent to the drill area.
- The coach is positioned outside the triangle and beside the ballcarrier.
- On the coach's command, the ballcarrier runs at three-quarter speed to the inside of the cone designated by the coach.
- The tackler reacts to the run of the ballcarrier and executes the angle tackle.
- The drill continues until all participants have had a sufficient number of repetitions.

Coaching Points:

- Always make sure tacklers are in a good *football position*.
- Instruct the ballcarriers to stay high, providing a good target for the tacklers.
- Make sure tacklers lead with the near foot, keeping their head up and eyes focused on the ballcarrier.
- Emphasize the importance of making contact on the rise (*throw uppercuts*) and *grabbing cloth* (to ensure no spin-outs) on all tackles.
- Make sure all tacklers practice the proper fundamentals and techniques of safe tackling.

Safety Considerations:

- A proper warm-up should precede drill.
- Full equipment should be worn.
- The drill should progress from form work to full speed. Instruct tacklers to never take the ballcarrier to the ground.
- The coach should watch for and eliminate all unacceptable match-ups as to size and athletic ability.
- The coach should closely monitor the intensity of the drill.
- Instruct all tacklers in the proper fundamentals and techniques of safe tackling.

Variation:

- Can be used as a form tackling or full-speed tackling drill (never live tackling).

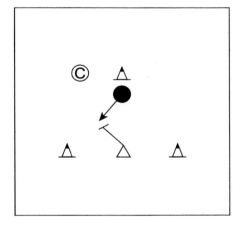

DOOR DRILL

Bob Otolski
Indiana State University, Illinois State University

Objective: To teach and practice the proper fundamentals and techniques of tackling.

Equipment Needed: Standard door, two cones, and footballs

Description:

- Position a standard door fitted with supports in an upright position on a selected line of scrimmage. A cone is placed three yards outside and two yards in front on each side of the door (see diagram).
- A row of tacklers is positioned four yards in front of and facing the door.
- A row of ballcarriers is aligned four yards in back of and facing the door.
- The coach stands adjacent to the drill area and, on his command, the first tackler *readies* himself as the ballcarrier sprints past either side of the door.
- As the ballcarrier runs into view, the tackler moves between the cone and the door and executes a shoulder tackle.
- The drill continues until all participants have had a sufficient number of tackles.

Coaching Points:

- Instruct all tacklers to keep their heads up, watching the ballcarrier's numbers.
- Special emphasis should be placed on the follow through.
- Make sure all tacklers practice the proper fundamentals and techniques of safe tackling.

Safety Considerations:

- It is imperative that a proper warm-up precede the drill.
- Instruct all personnel in the proper fundamentals and techniques of safe tackling.
- The coach should watch for and eliminate all unacceptable match-ups as to size and athletic ability.
- The drill should progress from form tackling to live tackling.
- The coach should closely monitor the intensity of the drill.
- A quick whistle is imperative with this drill.
- The training staff should be placed on special alert.

Variations:

- Can be used as a form or live tackling drill.
- Can vary the distances at which the tacklers line up from the front of the door.

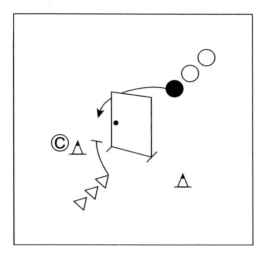

REBEL TACKLING

Billy Brewer
Southeastern Louisiana, Louisiana Tech University, University of Mississippi

Objective: To teach and practice the proper fundamentals and techniques of tackling. Skills related to agility, reaction, and explosion are also incorporated.

Equipment Needed: Three large blocking dummies and footballs

Description:

- Lay three blocking dummies in the letter "H" alignment shown in the diagram. The parameter of the drill area is five yards square.
- Position a row of tacklers on one side of the dummies and a row of ballcarriers on the opposite side.
- The coach stands adjacent to the drill area.
- On the coach's command, the first two drill participants take front-facing stances in front of the dummies on their respective sides.
- On the coach's second command, the ballcarrier and tackler shuffle right and left respectively and parallel to the horizontal dummies. They then *square* the corner where a form tackle is executed.
- The ballcarrier and tackler now retreat off the form tackle and the procedure is repeated to the other side.
- The procedure is repeated a third time with the tackler driving the ballcarrier back five yards.
- The drill continues until all participants have had a sufficient number of repetitions.

Coaching Points:

- Always check to see that personnel are in their proper stances.
- Make sure all tacklers maintain a square-shoulder relationship to the ballcarrier at all times.
- Instruct all tacklers to roll their hips and wrap their arms vigorously on all tackles.
- Make sure all tackles are made on the rise.
- Make sure that all personnel practice the proper fundamentals and techniques of safe tackling.

Safety Considerations:

- It is imperative that a proper warm-up precede the drill.
- Instruct all personnel in the proper fundamentals and techniques of safe tackling.
- The coach should watch for and eliminate all unacceptable match-ups as to size and athletic ability.
- The drill should progress from form to full-speed tackling (not live tackling).
- The coach should closely monitor the intensity of the drill.

Variations:

- Can be used as a form tackling or full-speed tackling drill (not live tackling).
- Can be used for both straight-on and angle tackling.
- Can have drill participants start from either up or down positions.
- Can be used with ballcarriers holding shields.

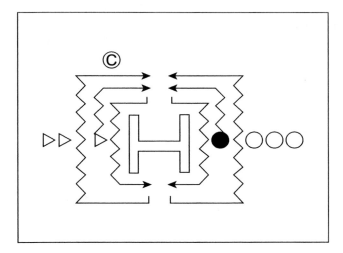

SHUFFLE TACKLE*

Barry Alvarez
University of Wisconsin
National Coach of the Year: 1993

Objective: To teach and practice the proper fundamentals and techniques of tackling. Incorporated are skills related to shuffling the feet, keeping the shoulders squared, keeping an inside-out leverage on the ballcarrier, and taking the correct angle to the ballcarrier when making a tackle.

Equipment Needed: Five large block dummies and hand shields

Description:

- Lay five block dummies two to two-and-a-half-yards apart and perpendicular to a selected line of scrimmage.

- Position a row of tacklers to the left of and one-and-a-half-yards behind and facing the row of dummies. Ballcarriers are aligned in a row, holding hand shields, in a similar position on the opposite side of the row of dummies (see diagram).

- On the coach's command, the first ballcarrier runs to the end of the row of dummies and back to the starting point.

- The tackler, shuffling his feet, mirrors the run of the ballcarrier to the end of the row of dummies and back.

- The ballcarrier now runs to and through any pair of the dummies as the tackler *buzzes* his feet and moves to tackle the ballcarrier.

- The drill continues until all the tacklers have had a sufficient number of repetitions from both left and right.

Coaching Points:

- Instruct the tacklers to maintain a good football position throughout the drill.

- After the tacklers have mirrored the ballcarrier back to the starting point, instruct the tacklers to *buzz* their feet and to be patient as they wait to see which pair of dummies the ballcarrier runs between.

- Instruct the tacklers to maintain a position on the backside hip of the ballcarrier and always approach him from an inside-out position, thus taking away the cutback angle.

- Make sure all the tacklers practice the proper fundamentals and techniques of safe tackling.

* Reprinted with permission from *101 Winning Football Drills: From the Legends of the Game* by Jerry Tolley

Safety Considerations:

- It is imperative that proper warm-up precedes this drill.
- Instruct all personnel in the proper fundamentals and technique of safe tackling.
- The drill should progress from form tackling to live tackling.
- The coach should monitor closely the intensity of the drill.
- The coach should watch for and eliminate all unacceptable match-ups as to size and athletic ability.

Variation:

- Can be used with ballcarriers holding hand shields for protection.

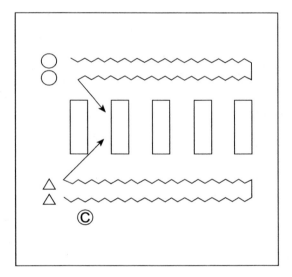

SCORE TACKLE

Serafino D. "Foge" Fazio
Boston University, Harvard University, University of Pittsburgh,
University of Cincinnati, University of Notre Dame,
Cleveland Browns, Minnesota Vikings, Atlanta Falcons,
New York Jets, Washington Redskins

Objective: To teach and practice the proper fundamentals and techniques of tackling with special emphasis placed on rolling the hips and wrapping the arms.

Equipment Needed: Two cones and footballs

Description:

- Align two cones five yards apart on the goal line.
- Position designated tacklers in a straight line behind the goal line side and the designated ballcarriers in a corresponding line facing the tacklers.
- The first tackler is aligned in a good football position with his heels on the goal line at the midpoint of the two cones. The first ballcarrier, holding a football, assumes a stance five yards in front of and facing the tackler.
- The coach stands adjacent to drill area.
- On the coach's command, the ballcarrier runs for a score just inside either of the two cones.
- The tackler reacts to the movement of the ballcarrier, *shuffles* down the goal line, and executes a form tackle.
- The drill continues until all participants have had a sufficient number of repetitions.

Coaching Points:

- Always check to see that tacklers are in a good *football position*.
- Under no circumstances is cross-over stepping allowed.
- Make sure that the tacklers' heads are up and are positioned across the body of the ballcarrier when contact is made.
- Special emphasis should be placed on rolling the hips and wrapping the arms on all tackles. (This can be encouraged by having the tacklers pull the ballcarrier toward them as the tackle is being executed)
- Make sure all tacklers practice the proper fundamentals and techniques of safe tackling.

Safety Considerations:

- It is imperative that a proper warm-up precede the drill.
- Instruct all personnel in the proper fundamentals and techniques of safe tackling.
- The coach should watch for and eliminate all unacceptable match-ups as to size and athletic ability.
- The drill should progress from form tackling to full-speed tackling (not live tackling).
- The coach should closely monitor the intensity of the drill.
- Instruct the tackler never to take the ballcarrier to the ground.

Variations:

- Can be used as a form tackling or full-speed tackling drill (not live tackling).
- Can be used with tacklers aligned with their backs to the ballcarrier.

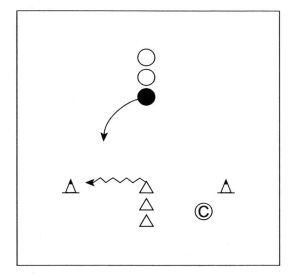

SHED TACKLING

> ## Thomas W. Throckmorton
> North Carolina State University, University of Richmond,
> Virginia Military Institute, East Carolina University, Virginia Polytechnic Institute,
> Wake Forest University, Boston College,
> The College of William and Mary, Houston Texans

Objective: To teach and practice the proper fundamentals and techniques of shedding a block and executing a tackle.

Equipment Needed: Hand shields and footballs

Description:

- Alternate designated blockers and ballcarriers in a straight line facing a row of designated tacklers. Three to five yards separate the first blocker and first tackler (see diagram).
- The blockers and ballcarriers work in pairs, with the blocker positioned in front holding a hand shield.
- The coach stands adjacent to drill area.
- On the coach's command, the first tackler takes on and defeats the block of the charging blocker.
- On the coach's second command, the first ballcarrier runs *up the hole* as the defender execute the tackle.
- The drill continues until all participants have had a sufficient number of tackles.

Coaching Points:

- Always check to see that tacklers are in their proper stances.
- Insist that all tacklers defeat the blockers and not just run around their head.
- Make sure all tacklers practice the proper fundamentals and techniques of safe tackling.

Safety Considerations:

- It is imperative that a proper warm-up precede the drill.
- Instruct all personnel in the proper fundamentals and techniques of safe tackling.
- The coach should watch for and eliminate all unacceptable match-ups as to size and athletic ability.
- The drill should progress from form tackling to live tackling.
- The coach should closely monitor the intensity of the drill.
- A quick whistle is imperative with this drill.
- The training staff should be placed on special alert.

Variation:

- Can be used as a form tackling or live tackling drill.

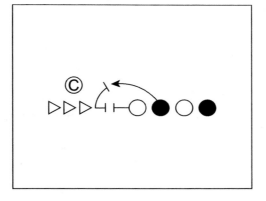

TACKLING DRILL*

Eddie Robinson
Grambling State University
National Black College Champions: 1955, 1967, 1972, 1974,
1975, 1977, 1980, 1983, and 1992
National Coach of the Year: 1992
National Black College Coach of the Year: 1967, 1972, 1974,
1975, 1977, 1980, 1983, and 1995
College Football Hall of Fame: 1997
Amos Alonzo Stagg Award: 1982
Tuss McLaughry Award: 1996
AFCA President: 1976

Objective: To teach and practice the proper fundamentals and techniques of tackling. Incorporated are skills related to reaction, agility, and quickness.

Equipment Needed: Five large blocking dummies and footballs

Description:

- Lay five blocking dummies three feet apart on a selected line of scrimmage (see diagram).

- Position a line of tacklers adjacent to the row of dummies and a row of ballcarriers seven yards in front of and facing the tacklers.

- The coach, holding a football, stands four yards in front of the ballcarriers.

- On the coach's command, the first tackler positions himself flat on his back with his head toward the first ballcarrier.

- On the cadence and snap count, the coach pitches the football to the first ballcarrier, who runs to the end of the dummy area and cuts upfield.

- The tackler reacts to the coach's cadence, springs to his feet, shuffles over and through the dummies and executes a tackle on the running back.

- The drill continues until all the tacklers have had a sufficient number of repetitions, shuffling over and through the dummies from both left and right alignment.

* Reprinted with permission from *101 Winning Football Drills: From the Legends of the Game* by Jerry Tolley

Coaching Points:

- Make sure the tacklers maintain a good football position as they shuffle over and through the dummies. Cross-over stepping should be discouraged.
- Make sure the tacklers practice proper fundamentals and techniques of safe tackling.
- The tackle should be viewed from various angles.
- Insist that tacklers shuffle through the dummies at full speed.

Safety Considerations:

- It is imperative that a proper warm-up precede this drill.
- The drill should progress from form tackling to live tackling.
- The coach should monitor closely the intensity of the drill.
- The coach should watch for and eliminate all unacceptable match-ups as to size and athletic ability.
- Instruct all tacklers in the proper fundamentals and techniques of safe tackling.
- The training staff should be placed on special alert.

Variations:

- Can be used as a form tackling or live tackling drill.
- Can be used with a lead blocker and ballcarrier.
- Can be used with a player holding a hand dummy and jamming the tackler as he gets off the ground.

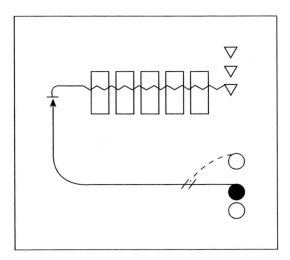

TWO-ON-ONE HIT DRILL

Robert F. Shoup
California Lutheran College, University of New Mexico, Ventura College
National Champions: California Lutheran 1971
National Coach of the Year: California Lutheran 1972

Objective: To teach and practice the proper fundamentals and techniques of tackling.

Equipment Needed: Two cones and footballs

Description:

- Place two cones 10 yards apart on a selected line of scrimmage.
- Align paired tacklers at an equal distance apart between cones and just behind the line of scrimmage (see diagram).
- Other tacklers stand adjacent to the drill area.
- A row of ballcarriers is positioned five yards in front of paired tacklers.
- The coach stands adjacent to the drill area.
- On the coach's command, the first ballcarrier *jockeys* back and forth between the cones as the paired tacklers slide with the ballcarrier's movements. Tacklers are instructed to keep an inside-outside relationship to the ballcarrier.
- After moving back and forth a few times, the ballcarrier attempts to cross the line of scrimmage as both defenders move to make the tackle.
- Tacklers should work from both the left and right sides of the drill.
- The drill continues until all paired tacklers have had a sufficient number of repetitions.

Coaching Points:

- Insist that tacklers keep their shoulders parallel to the line of scrimmage throughout the drill.
- Make sure paired tacklers maintain an equal distance between them as they slide back and forth behind the line of scrimmage.
- Make sure all tacklers practice the proper fundamentals and techniques of safe tackling.

Safety Considerations:

- It is imperative that a proper warm-up precede the drill.
- Instruct all personnel in the proper fundamentals and techniques of safe tackling (keep the helmet out of the tackle).
- The coach should watch for and eliminate all unacceptable match-ups as to size and athletic ability.
- The coach should closely monitor the intensity of the drill.
- A quick whistle is imperative with this drill.
- The training staff should be placed on special alert.

Variations:

- Can be used as a motivation drill by keeping count of successful offensive and defensive performances.
- Can use the sideline as the selected line of scrimmage and set up multiple drill stations.
- Can be used as a running back drill.

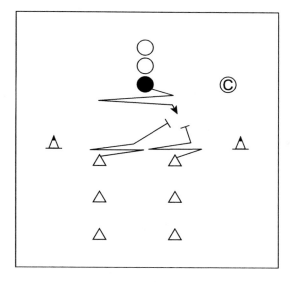

TACKLING CIRCUIT

Kirk Ferentz
University of Maine, Cleveland Browns, Baltimore Ravens, University of Iowa
National Coach of the Year: Iowa 2002

Objective: To teach and practice the proper fundamentals and techniques of tackling.

Equipment Needed: Seven agile dummies, five cones, and a football

Description:

- Divide all defensive players into four tackling units (defensive tackles and larger defensive ends; outside linebackers and smaller defensive ends; inside linebackers; defensive backs).
- A defensive coach is assigned to each tackling station.
- It is recommended that this drill be done daily by all defensive players following the stretching period.
- All defensive players rotate through each tackling station, spending two minutes at each station as noted below.
  - *Shoots Drill*
    - Place two agile dummies approximately two yards apart on a selected line of scrimmage (see diagram A).
    - Position a tackler in the *football position* and a ballcarrier in a front-facing alignment three yards apart and midway between the two dummies.
    - Other drill participants should stand adjacent to the drill area.
    - On the coach's command, the ballcarrier runs forward and the tackler reacts to the ballcarrier's run and executes the form tackle.
  - *Eye Opener Drill*
    - Place five agile dummies one yard apart on a selected line of scrimmage.
    - Position a tackler in the *football position* and a ballcarrier in a front-facing alignment five yards apart and adjacent to the row of dummies. Tacklers are aligned beside the row of dummies (see diagram B).
    - Other drill participants should stand adjacent to the drill area.
    - On the coach's command the ballcarrier runs down the line of agile dummies and cuts upfield and runs through any two of the dummies.
    - The tackler reacts to the run of the ballcarrier and shuffles over and through the dummies, mirroring the run of the ballcarrier, and executes the form tackle.
    - The drill should be conducted from both a left and right tackling alignment.

- *Angle Tackling Drill*
  - Place three cones to form an equilateral triangle. Five yards separate each of the three cones (see diagram C).
  - Position a ballcarrier in front of the cone that forms the apex of the triangle.
  - Align a tackler in the *football position* midway between the cones that form the base of the triangle.
  - Other drill participants stand adjacent to the drill area.
  - On the coach's command, the ballcarrier moves forward and cuts either left or right.
  - The tackler reacts to the run of the ballcarrier and executes the form tackle.
- *Sideline Tackling Drill*
  - Place two cones 10 yards apart and two yards from a selected sideline.
  - Position a tackler in the *football position* midway between the cones and five yards from the sideline.
  - Position a ballcarrier in front of the front cone (see diagram D).
  - Other drill participants should stand adjacent to the drill area.
  - On the coach's command, the ballcarrier runs straight down the sideline.
  - The tackler reacts to the run of the ballcarrier and executes the form tackle.
  - The drill should be conducted from both a left and right tackling alignment.

Coaching Points:

- Always check to see that all tacklers begin each drill execution from a good *football position*.
- Emphasize the importance of keeping the head up, eyes open, and executing the tackle on the rise.
- Instruct tacklers to roll the hips, wrap the arms, and follow through on all form tackles.
- On the Eye Opener Drill, instruct the tackler to always maintain a back-hip relationship to the ballcarrier and execute the tackle from an inside-out alignment.
- On the Angle Tackling Drill, instruct the tacklers that, in closing the gap on the ballcarrier, they should step toward his cut and always keep the head up and in front.
- On the Sideline Tackling Drill, instruct the tacklers to utilize the sideline to their advantage and to tackle through the shoulder of the ballcarrier.
- Make sure all tacklers practice the proper fundamentals and techniques of safe tackling.

Safety Considerations:

- A proper warm-up should precede the drill.
- The drill areas should be clear of all foreign articles. This includes the sideline area.
- Make sure an adequate distance is maintained between the different tackling stations.
- This drill is only to be used as a form-tackling drill.
- Instruct all tacklers in the proper fundamentals and techniques of safe tackling.
- Instruct the tacklers to never bring the ballcarrier to the ground.

A

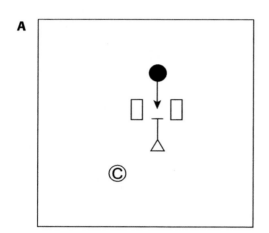

B

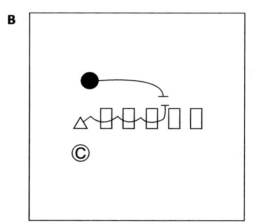

C

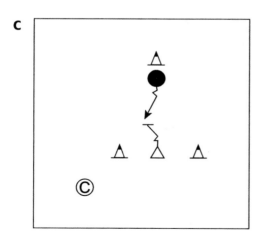

D

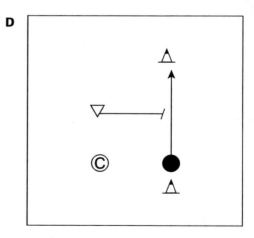

6

Defensive Pursuit Drills

DOUBLE HUSTLE DRILL

George W. Elliott
Northeastern Oklahoma State University

Objective: To teach and practice total team pursuit with special emphasis placed on rushing the passer, reacting to a thrown pass, and blocking for an interception. This drill can also be used to build cardiovascular endurance.

Equipment Needed: Five large blocking dummies and a football

Description:

- Align the defensive unit in a huddle over the football behind a selected line of scrimmage.
- Other defensive units are positioned adjacent to the drill area.
- A quarterback (coach) is positioned over the football.
- Five held dummies are placed seven yards apart on a yard line 10 yards behind the defensive line.
- A receiver is positioned at the line of scrimmage on each sideline (see diagram).
- On the defensive signal caller's command, all defensive personnel break from the huddle and take their normal positions over the football.
- The coach calls cadence and simulates a ball snap as the defense reacts. He then either passes the football to the receiver on one of the sidelines or drops back and throws a pass downfield.
- If the coach throws the football to a receiver on the sideline, the entire defensive unit pursues that receiver as he sprints down the field.
- If the coach drops back to throw a downfield pass, the defensive front rushes him, while the linebackers and defensive backs drop to their respective pass coverage zones.
- When the football is thrown, all defensive personnel sprint toward the football for a possible interception. After the interception is made, the defensive linemen execute blocks on the standup dummies, and all other defensive personnel sprint past the line of scrimmage.
- The drill continues with alternating defensive units pursuing both left and right or reacting to an intercepted pass.

Coaching Points:

- Always check to see that all defensive personnel are aligned correctly and are in their proper stances.
- Make sure all defenders take their proper pursuit angles.
- Insist that all defensive personnel pursue the football at full speed.

Safety Considerations:

- A proper warm-up should precede the drill.
- The drill area should be clear of all foreign articles. This includes the sideline areas.
- Maintain a minimum distance of seven yards between held dummies.
- Dummy holders should be instructed to release dummies as the blocks are being executed.
- When used as a conditioning drill, the coach should closely monitor the fatigue level of all drill participants throughout the drill period.
- This drill should not be used as a conditioning exercise during extreme heat or high humidity conditions.
- When used as a conditioning drill, the training staff should be placed on special alert.

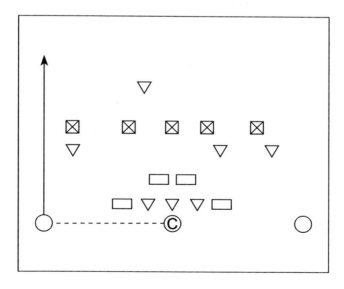

PERFECT PLAY PURSUIT DRILL

Charley B. Pell (Deceased)
University of Alabama, University of Kentucky, Virginia Polytechnic Institute, Jacksonville State University, Clemson University, University of Florida

---

Objective: To teach and practice total team pursuit against both running and passing plays.

Equipment Needed: Four cones and a football

Description:

- Align a defensive unit in a huddle over the football behind a selected line of scrimmage.
- Other defensive units are positioned adjacent to drill area.
- A quarterback (coach) is positioned over the football.
- Three cones are placed seven yards apart on a yard line 15 yards behind the defensive line. A fourth cone is placed seven yards behind and to the left of the quarterback (coach).
- A receiver is positioned at the line of scrimmage on each sideline (see diagram).
- On the defensive signal caller's command, all defensive personnel break the huddle and take their normal positions over the football.
- The coach calls cadence and simulates a snap by slapping the football. He then either passes the football to the receiver on one of the sidelines or drops back to throw a pass downfield.
- If the coach passes the football to a receiver on the sideline, the entire defensive unit pursues that receiver as he sprints down the field.
- If the coach drops back to pass the football downfield, the defensive front rushes him, sprinting past the single cone behind the line of scrimmage. The linebackers and defensive backs drop to their respective pass coverage zones.
- When the football is thrown, all defensive personnel sprint toward the football for a possible interception. As the football is being intercepted, the defensive linemen sprint past the three cones stationed downfield, and all other defensive personnel sprint past the line of scrimmage.
- The drill continues with alternating defensive units pursuing both left and right or defending against the pass.

Coaching Points:

- Always check to see that all defensive personnel are aligned correctly and are in their proper stances.

- Make sure all defensive personnel take their proper pursuit angles.

- Insist that all defensive personnel pursue the football at full speed.

- The following criteria are considered in deciding if the defense pursued perfectly: huddle break, the defensive front sprinting past both cone stations, secondary dropping into proper pass coverage zones, intercepting the thrown pass, and all-out sprinting by all defensive personnel past the sideline on running plays and the secondary sprinting past the line of scrimmage on pass plays.

Safety Considerations:

- A proper warm-up should precede the drill.

- The drill area should be clear of all foreign articles. This includes sideline areas.

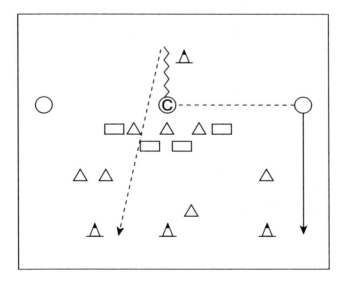

PURSUIT DRILL

Charlie E. Forbes
Guilford College, Lenoir Rhyne College

Objective: To teach and practice total team pursuit. This drill can also be used to build cardiovascular endurance.

Equipment Needed: Footballs

Description:

- Align a defensive unit in a huddle over the football behind a selected line of scrimmage.
- Other defensive units are positioned adjacent to the drill area.
- A quarterback (coach) is positioned over the football.
- A receiver is positioned at the line of scrimmage on each sideline (see diagram).
- On the defensive signal caller's command, all defensive personnel break from the huddle and take their normal positions over the football.
- The coach calls out an imaginary offensive set and then calls cadence and simulates a ball snap. The defensive personnel react to the simulated ball snap.
- The coach then runs through the steps of an imaginary offensive play and either throws the football to the receiver on either sideline or places the football at any point on the ground.
- If the coach throws the ball to a receiver on a sideline, the entire defensive unit pursues that receiver as he sprints down the field.
- If he places the football on the ground, all defensive personnel sprint to the football and assume the break-down position. Then, on the coach's whistle, all defenders sprint back to their pre-play huddle positions.
- The drill continues with alternating defensive units pursuing both left and right or breaking down on a placed football.

Coaching Points:

- Always check to see that all personnel are aligned correctly and are in their proper stances.
- Check to see that the initial steps of all defenders are congruent with the defense called in the huddle.
- Make sure all defenders take their proper pursuit angles.
- Insist that all personnel pursue to the football at full speed.

Safety Considerations:

- A proper warm-up should precede the drill.
- The drill area should be cleared of all foreign articles. This includes sideline areas.
- When used as a conditioning drill, the coach should closely monitor the fatigue level of all drill participants throughout the drill period.
- This drill should not be used as a conditioning exercise during extreme heat or high humidity conditions.
- When used as a conditioning drill, the training staff should be placed on special alert.

Variations:

- Can place standup dummies at various points on each sideline and designate certain pursuers as dummy tacklers.
- Can throw the football to a receiver at different positions up the sideline or to receivers at various spots on the football field.

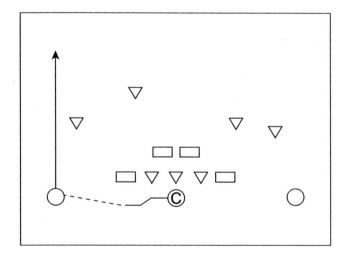

TEAM PURSUIT DRILL

William "Jim" Fuller
Jacksonville State University, University of Alabama

Objective: To teach and practice total team pursuit. This drill can also be used to build cardiovascular endurance.

Equipment Needed: Footballs

Description:

- Align a defensive unit in a huddle over the football behind a selected line of scrimmage.
- Other defensive units are positioned adjacent to drill area.
- A quarterback is positioned over the football.
- Seven ballcarriers are placed in specific alignments on the football field (see diagram).
- On defensive signal caller's command, all defensive personnel break from the huddle and take their normal positions over the football.
- The quarterback calls cadence and simulates a ball snap as the defensive team reacts.
- Then the quarterback either pitches the football to one of the ballcarriers aligned at the running back positions or passes the football to one of the other five designated ballcarriers.
- If one of the ballcarriers aligned in the running back position receives the football, he runs a sweep action. The entire defensive unit pursues his movements and breaks down in a *football position* around him. Then, on the coach's whistle, all defensive personnel sprint back to their pre-play huddle positions.
- If the quarterback throws the football to one of the other five ballcarriers, that ballcarrier remains stationary as all defensive personnel react and move in the same manner described in the previous point.
- The drill continues with alternating defensive units pursuing to any one of the seven designated areas.

Coaching Points:

- Always check to see that all defensive personnel are aligned correctly and are in their proper stances.
- Make sure all defensive personnel take their proper pursuit angles.
- Insist that all defensive personnel pursue to the football at full speed.
- Team excellence should be stressed throughout the drill including huddle discipline and break, contain and pursuit principles, and return to huddle.

Safety Considerations:

- A proper warm-up should precede the drill.
- The drill area should be clear of all foreign articles.
- When used as a conditioning drill, the coach should closely monitor the fatigue level of all defensive personnel throughout the drill period.
- The drill should not be used as a conditioning exercise during extreme heat or high humidity conditions.
- When used as a conditioning drill, the training staff should be placed on special alert.

Variations:

- Can allow a pitch-receiving ballcarrier to sprint down the sideline as defenders take their proper pursuit angles.
- Can allow defenders to intercept the pass, creating a sudden change situation.

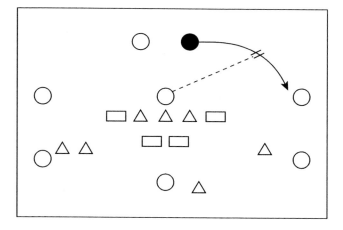

SIDELINE TEAM PURSUIT DRILL

Vic Rowen
Defiance College, San Francisco State University

Objective: To teach and practice total team pursuit.

Equipment Needed: Footballs

Description:

- Align a defensive unit in a huddle over the football behind a selected line of scrimmage.
- Other defensive units are positioned adjacent to drill area.
- A quarterback (coach) is positioned over the football. Another coach is placed at the line of scrimmage on each sideline (see diagram).
- The quarterback (coach) calls the defensive front and coverage. The defensive personnel break the huddle and take their normal positions over the football.
- The quarterback (coach) calls cadence and simulates a ball snap as the defensive unit reacts and runs in place.
- Then the quarterback (coach) points the football to either sideline and the entire defensive unit pursues the coach standing on the sideline as he sprints down the field.
- The drill continues until alternating defensive units have had a sufficient number of repetitions pursuing both left and right.

Coaching Points:

- Always check to see that all defensive personnel are aligned correctly and are in their proper stances.
- Make sure all defensive personnel take their proper pursuit angles.
- Insist that all defensive personnel pursue the football at full speed.

Safety Considerations:

- A proper warm-up should precede the drill.
- The drill area should be clear of all foreign articles. This includes sideline areas.

Variations:

- Can be run from various positions on the field.
- Quarterback (coach) can execute a pass drop and the defense can react accordingly.

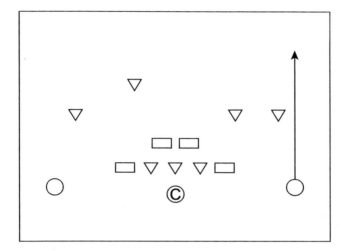

TEAM PURSUIT OVER OBSTACLES

S. S. "Red" Wilson
Elon University, Duke University

Objective: To teach and practice total team pursuit. This drill can also be used to build cardiovascular endurance.

Equipment Needed: A football and all available shields and dummies

Description:

- Align a defensive unit in a huddle over the football behind a selected line of scrimmage.
- Other defensive units are positioned adjacent to drill area.
- A quarterback (coach) is positioned over the football.
- A row of ballcarriers is placed five yards deep behind the coach.
- Lay all available shields and dummies in a pattern 10 yards by 10 yards adjacent to the defense. The shields and dummies should be placed in such a way that all defenders must shuffle over them as they pursue the ballcarrier.
- On the defensive signal caller's command, all defensive personnel break from the huddle and take their normal positions over the football.
- The coach calls cadence and simulates a ball snap as the defense reacts.
- The coach pitches the football to the first ballcarrier, who runs a wide sweep play.
- The entire defensive unit reacts to the play and pursues the ballcarrier over and through the gauntlet of shields and dummies.
- When the coach blows his whistle to conclude the drill, all pursuers come to a sudden stop and the coach checks for proper pursuit angles.
- The drill continues with alternating defensive units pursuing both left and right over the shields and dummies.

Coaching Points:

- Always check to see that all defensive personnel are aligned correctly and are in proper stances.
- Make sure all defensive personnel take their proper pursuit angles.
- Instruct all defensive personnel to keep their shoulders parallel to the line of scrimmage as they run the gauntlet of shields and dummies.
- Insist that all defensive personnel pursue to the football at full speed.

Safety Considerations:

- A proper warm-up should precede the drill.
- Players with knee problems should be excused from this drill.
- When used as a conditioning drill, the coach should closely monitor the fatigue level of all drill participants throughout the drill period.
- The drill should not be used as a conditioning exercise during extreme heat or high humidity conditions.
- When used as a conditioning drill, the training staff should be placed on special alert.

Variations:

- Can be used without shields and dummies.
- Can be used with the quarterback (coach) passing the football to a stationary receiver downfield.

7

General Agility Drills

BULLNECK DRILL*

Wayne "Woody" Hayes (Deceased)
Denison University, Miami University (OH), The Ohio State University
National Champions: Ohio State 1954, 1957, 1961, 1968, and 1970
National Coach of the Year: Ohio State 1957, 1968, and 1975
College Football Hall of Fame: 1983
Amos Alonzo Stagg Award: 1986
AFCA President: 1963

Objective: To stretch and strengthen the muscles of the neck.

Equipment Needed: None

Description:

- Align all the squad members in calisthenics lines.

- The drill coordinator is positioned in front of the team.

- On the drill coordinator's command, all players pair up on pre-designated yard lines. One of the paired players is positioned on his hands and knees facing the drill coordinator. The other partner stands adjacent to him.

- On the drill coordinator's command, the standing player places his clasped hands behind the head of his partner. From this position, an isometric contraction is executed for five to eight seconds with the down partner's head resisting the pulling forward action of his partner.

- The procedure is repeated with the standing player pushing against the right and then the left sides of his partner's head with the palms of his hands.

- Now the standing player clasps his hands under the chin of his partner and pulls upward. The down-drill participant again offers strong resistance.

- The drill participants now change places and the procedures are repeated.

---

* Reprinted with permission from *101 Winning Football Drills: From the Legends of the Game* by Jerry Tolley

---

Coaching Points:

- Instruct all the drill participants to start and stop all procedures on the drill coordinator's commands.

- Insist that all down-drill participants hold their heads *way up* as high as they can get it.

Safety Considerations:

- The pressure exerted by the standing partner never should be great enough to force his partner's head out of its original position.

- The pressure applied by the standing partner should be increased gradually from day to day.

COMBINATION BAG AGILITY DRILL

Joe W. McDaniel
Muskingum College, Marietta College, Centre College

Objective: To develop general agility, footwork, and body control. Skills related to moving laterally and recovering a fumble are also incorporated.

Equipment Needed: Five large blocking dummies and footballs

Description:

- Lay five dummies one yard apart and perpendicular to a selected line of scrimmage (see diagram).
- Position a row of players adjacent to the dummy area.
- The coach stands at the starting point of the drill and a manager with a football stands at the other end.
- On the coach's command, the first drill participant assumes the *football position* in front of the row of dummies while working his feet. Then, on the coach's hand signal, he *shuffles* laterally over and through the gauntlet of dummies, chopping his feet and keeping his shoulders squared to the line of scrimmage.
- After stepping over the final dummy, the drill participant stands in place while working his feet.
- The manager then rolls the football on the ground and the player recovers the fumble.
- The drill continues until all personnel have had a sufficient number of repetitions.
- The drill should be conducted to both the left and right.

Coaching Points:

- Insist that all players maintain the proper *football position* throughout the drill.
- Make sure that all players keep their shoulders squared and their center of gravity low as they *shuffle* laterally over and through the dummies.
- Encourage drill participants to work their feet as quickly as possible.
- Make sure players practice the proper fundamentals and techniques of recovering a fumble.

Safety Considerations:

- A proper warm-up should precede the drill.
- Instruct all personnel in the proper fundamentals and techniques of recovering a fumble.
- Players with knee problems should be excused from this drill.

Variation:

- Can have drill participants move around each dummy instead of over and through them (forward, laterally, backward, laterally, forward, etc.).

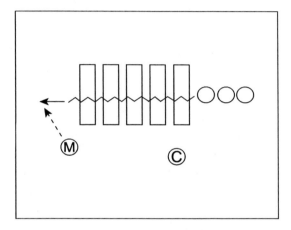

FOUR-CORNER DRILL*

Glenn "Bo" Schembechler
Miami University (OH), University of Michigan
National Coach of the Year: Michigan 1969 and 1977
College Football Hall of Fame: 1993
Amos Alonzo Stagg Award: 1999
AFCA President: 1983

Objective: To develop general agility, flexibility, quickness, coordination, and reaction.

Equipment Needed: Four cones

Description:

- Align four cones five yards apart in a square (see diagram).
- Position the drill participants in a straight line behind one of the cones.
- The coach stands adjacent to the start-finish area.
- On the coach's command, the first drill participant drives out of his stance and *bear crawls* to the first cone. He then stands up and faces the outside of the drill area and *cariocas* to the second cone. He now *runs backward* to the third cone, and then turns and *sprints* past the fourth cone.
- The drill continues until all the drill participants have had a sufficient number of repetitions.
- The drill should be conducted in both clockwise and counterclockwise directions.

Coaching Points:

- Always check to see that all the personnel start the drill in their proper stances.
- Instruct the drill participants to get their arms and legs up under them when they execute the *bear crawl*.
- Make sure the players maintain the desired body positions throughout the drill.
- Insist that the drill be conducted at full speed.
- Instruct the drill participants to sprint past the fourth cone.

* Reprinted with permission from *101 Winning Football Drills: From the Legends of the Game* by Jerry Tolley

Safety Considerations:

- A proper warm-up should precede the drill.
- Maintain a minimum distance of five yards between performing drill participants.
- Instruct all the personnel as to the proper techniques of executing the *bear crawl* and *carioca*.
- The players with knee problems should be excused from the *carioca* and backward run portions of this drill.

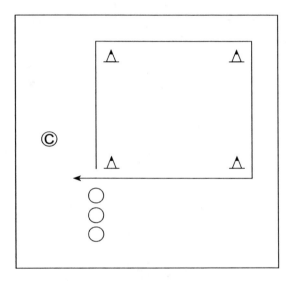

FOLLOW-THE-LEADER DRILL

Dwight D. "Mickey" Brown
Elon University, Duke University

Objective: To develop general agility, reaction, and quickness.

Equipment Needed: Four cones

Description:

- Align four cones three yards apart in a square. The cones are designated A, B, C, and D as shown in the diagram.
- Position drill participants in equal lines behind cones A and C.
- The coach stands adjacent to the drill area.
- On the coach's instructions, the first two drill participants step inside the square and assume a *football position*. The players behind cone A are designated leaders and the players behind cone C are designated followers.
- On the coach's command, the leader shuffles in one of the following patterns as the follower reacts and shuffles in the opposite direction:
  - When the leader moves to cone B, the follower moves to cone D.
  - When the leader moves to cone D, the follower moves to cone B.
  - When the leader moves to cone C, the follower moves to cone A.
- The movement pattern continues at the discretion of the leader for approximately 10 seconds before the participants go to opposite lines.
- The drill continues until all participants have had a sufficient number of repetitions both as leader and follower.

Coaching Points:

- Insist that drill participants maintain a good *football position*, working their feet, throughout the drill.
- Players should be instructed never to use cross-over steps.
- Instruct all personnel to execute their movement patterns as quickly as possible.

Safety Considerations:

- A proper warm-up should precede the drill.
- When crossing from A to C, drill participants should be instructed to stay to their right.
- Players with knee problems should be excused from this drill.

Variation:

- Can start the drill with players lying on their backs.

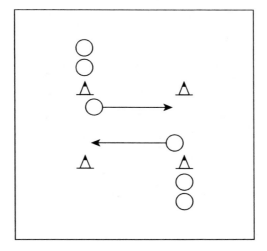

MIRROR DRILL*

Paul F. Dietzel
Louisiana State University, United States Military Academy,
University of South Carolina
National Champions: Louisiana State 1958
National Coach of the Year: Louisiana State 1958
AFCA President: 1969

Objective: To develop general agility, quickness, coordination, and reaction time. Incorporated are skills related to recovering a fumble.

Equipment Needed: Footballs

Description:

- Align a ballcarrier, holding a football, in a front-facing position toward two pursuing players. Five yards separate the ballcarrier from the first pursuer. The second pursuer lines up three yards behind the first pursuer (see diagram).

- This drill alignment can be repeated at various positions on the field.

- On the coach's command, the ballcarrier moves quickly either to his left or right, while the two pursuers mirror his moves while maintaining a squared-shoulder relationship to him.

- The ballcarrier continues with various movement patterns including forward and sideward rolls in an attempt to lose the pursuers.

- Finally, after four to six movement patterns have been executed, the ballcarrier fumbles the football and moves clear.

- The pursuers yell *ball - ball* and move to recover the loose football.

- The drill continues until all the drill participants have had a sufficient number of repetitions both as ballcarriers and as pursuers.

Coaching Points:

- Insist that all the pursuers keep their shoulders squared toward the ballcarrier at all times.

- Instruct ballcarriers to make short, abrupt changes in direction.

* Reprinted with permission from *101 Winning Football Drills: From the Legends of the Game* by Jerry Tolley

Safety Considerations:

- A proper warm-up should precede the drill.
- Maintain a safe distance between the three drill participants.
- Instruct all personnel in the proper techniques of recovering a fumble.
- Instruct the first pursuer to reach the fumbled football to make the recovery and assign the second pursuer to protect him.
- If the players are not in full gear, do not execute the fumble and fumble recovery.

Variation:

- Encourage the ballcarriers to use their imagination in trying to elude the pursuers.

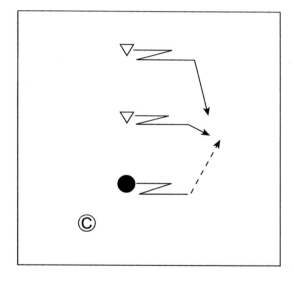

FOUR-POINT WAVE-SEAT ROLL

Ronald Albert "Ron" Rogerson (Deceased)
Colorado State University, Lebanon Valley College,
University of Delaware, University of Maine, Princeton University

Objective: To develop general agility, quickness, and reaction time. Skills related to getting up off the ground and assuming a football position are also incorporated.

Equipment Needed: None

Description:

- Align three rows of players three yards apart behind a selected line of scrimmage as shown in the diagram.
- The coach is positioned in front of the drill participants.
- On the coach's command, the first wave of drill participants jumps into four-point stances.
- The coach then directs the players to move either left or right by pointing his hand. He also can instruct players to execute seat rolls by pointing his right or left hand to the ground.
- After six or eight movements have been executed, the players are instructed to jump off the ground and assume a good *football position*.
- The drill continues until all participants have had a sufficient number of repetitions.

Coaching Points:

- Instruct drill participants to keep the head, shoulders, hips, and feet parallel to the line of scrimmage throughout the drill.
- Make sure all players react to the coach's hand signals correctly and as quickly as possible.
- Insist that drill participants move at full speed when getting off the ground and assuming the *football position*.

Safety Considerations:

- A proper warm-up should precede the drill.
- Maintain a minimum distance of three yards between performing drill participants.

Variations:

- Can have drill participants execute either the wave or seat roll.
- Can incorporate a forward roll and a 10-yard sprint to end the drill.
- Can be used as a conditioning drill.

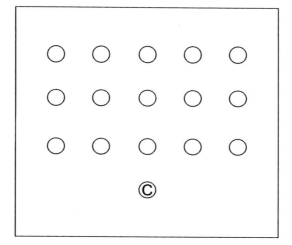

WAVE DRILL*

Charles "Cholly Mac" McClendon (Deceased)
Louisiana State University
National Coach of the Year: 1970
College Football Hall of Fame: 1986
Amos Alonzo Stagg Award: 1992
AFCA President: 1979
AFCA Executive Director: 1982-1994

Objective: To develop general agility, concentration, reaction, body control, sense of direction, and competitiveness. Incorporated are skills related to recovering a fumble.

Equipment Needed: Footballs

Description:

- Align two players in a *football position* five yards apart on the five-yard line. Players face the sideline.
- A third player designated the leader stands five yards in front and faces the two players designated the followers (see diagram).
- The left and right boundaries of the drill area are the goal line and 10-yard line.
- Other drill participants stand on the sideline.
- The coach stands adjacent to the drill area with a football in hand.
- On the coach's command, the leader executes various movement patterns including cross-over steps left and right, side rolls left and right, squats, ground touches, jumps into air with arms raised over head, and forward rolls (forward rolls should be executed vertically to the five-yard line).
- The followers try to mirror the exact movement patterns of the leader while maintaining a nose-to-nose relationship to him.
- The drill is concluded when the coach pitches the football outside the drill area and yells *ball - ball*. All the drill participants now try to recover the loose football.
- The drill continues until all the drill participants have had a sufficient number of repetitions as both leaders and followers.

* Reprinted with permission from *101 Winning Football Drills: From the Legends of the Game* by Jerry Tolley

Coaching Points:

- Insist that all the followers keep their shoulders squared to an imaginary line of scrimmage throughout the drill.
- Instruct all the drill participants to execute their movement patterns as quickly as possible.
- This should be a fun drill done by all positions.
- This drill is not recommended as a conditioning drill.

Safety Considerations:

- A proper warm-up should precede the drill.
- Maintain a minimum distance of five-yards between each of the three drill participants.
- Instruct all the personnel in the proper techniques of recovering a fumble.
- The coach should monitor closely the intensity of the fumble recovery.

Variation:

- If players are not in full gear, a breakdown and a sprint out are substituted for the fumble recovery.

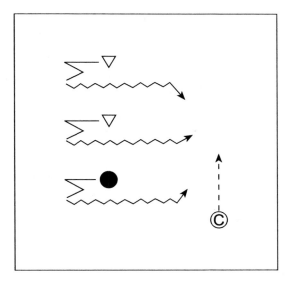

FOUR AND TWO*

Clarence Stasavich (Deceased)
[Drill submitted by David M. Alexander]
Lenoir-Rhyne College, East Carolina University
National Champions: Lenoir-Rhyne 1960
National Coach of the Year: Lenoir-Rhyne 1959; East Carolina 1964

Objective: To teach and practice various movement patterns and methods of catching the football. Incorporated are skills related to reaction, agility, and quickness.

Equipment Needed: Footballs

Description:

- Align the drill participants in a row perpendicular to a selected line of scrimmage.
- A quarterback, holding a football, is positioned 15 yards in front of the first drill participants (see diagram).
- On the quarterback's command, the first drill participant assumes the football position.
- On the quarterback's ball signal (shows pass), the first drill participant takes four steps up and two steps back and then cuts a 90-degree angle either left or right on quarterback's shoulder turn.
- The quarterback throws the pass to the drill participant who makes the interception and returns the football to the quarterback.
- The drill continues until all the drill participants have had a sufficient number of repetitions.
- The drill can be conducted with any number of drill stations.

Coaching Points:

- Insist that the drill participants maintain good body alignment throughout the drill.
- Instruct the drill participants to always watch the quarterback.
- Insist that the drill be conducted at full speed.

* Reprinted with permission from *101 Winning Football Drills: From the Legends of the Game* by Jerry Tolley

Safety Considerations:

- A proper warm-up should precede the drill.
- The drill area should be clear of all foreign articles.
- If more than one drill station is used, maintain a minimum distance of 25 yards between stations.

Variations:

- Can be used with the drill participants moving back at a 45-degree angle after they have completed their four-up and two-back stepping.
- Can be used with the drill participants executing a backpedal after their four-up, two-back, and 90-degree cut either left or right stepping.

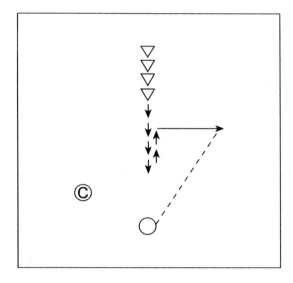

CONE DRILL*

Howard L. Schnellenberger
University of Miami, University of Louisville, The University of Oklahoma,
Baltimore Colts, Florida Atlantic University
National Champions: University of Miami 1983
National Coach of the Year: University of Miami 1983

Objective: To teach and practice the proper fundament of various movements related to football. Incorporated are skills related to reaction, agility, and quickness.

Equipment Needed: Four cones

Description:

- Place four cones seven yards apart to form a square.
- Position the drill participants in a straight line next to cone A as shown in the diagram.
- The drill is conducted in four phases and in a counterclockwise direction as noted in the following. The coach stands inside the square during the first two phases of the drill, and then moves outside the cones for the last two phases.
  - *Shuffle.* On the coach's command, the first drill participant assumes the *football position* facing cone A. On the coach's second command, he shuffles to cone B and executes a 90-degree left turn and sprints past cone C. The drill continues with the other drill participants taking their turns. The players now return to cone B.
  - *Step Around.* On the coach's command, the first drill participant assumes a three-point stance beside cone B and faces the outside of the drill area. On the coach's second command, he steps and pivots to the left touching cone B with his left hand. The drill participant now sprints to cone C, keeping his eyes on the coach who is still positioned inside the square. The drill continues with the other drill participants taking their turns.
  - *Backpedal.* On the coach's command, the first drill participant assumes the *football position* beside cone C with his back to cone D. The coach moves outside the drill area and takes a front-facing position to the drill participant. The

* Reprinted with permission from *101 Winning Football Drills: From the Legends of the Game* by Jerry Tolley

coach now attempts to place his hands on the drill participant's head. The drill participant reacts to the coach's hand movement and sprints backward past cone D. The drill continues with the other drill participants sprinting backward.

- *Scramble.* On the coach's command, the first drill participant assumes a three-point stance beside cone D and faces cone A. The coach is positioned midway between the two cones and faces the drill participant. On the coach's command, the drill participant sprints to the coach and then scrambles on *all fours* past cone A. The drill continues with other drill participants taking their turns.

- The four phases of the drill are now executed in a clockwise direction.

Coaching Points:

- Always check to see that the drill participants are in the correct *football position* or in their proper stances.
- In executing the *shuffle,* make sure that the drill participants keep their shoulders square to the cones and avoid crossover stepping.
- Make sure that all the drill participants keep their eyes on the coach as they execute the *step around* phase of the drill.
- In executing the *backpedal,* instruct the drill participants to use short, choppy steps and to keep the head up. They should also avoid false stepping as they initiate the backward run.
- Insist that the drill participants explode out of their stances and sprint to the coach before executing the *scramble.*
- Insist that the drill be conducted at full speed.

Safety Considerations:

- Proper warm-up should precede the drill.
- Players with knee problems should be excused from certain phases of this drill.

Variation:

- Can be used as an offensive line drill.

A

B

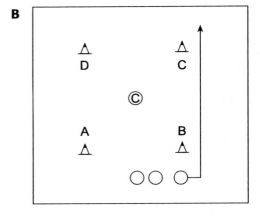

C

D

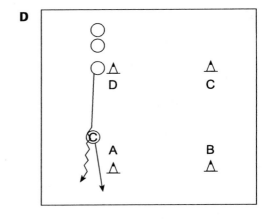

8

Drills for Developing and Maintaining Cardiovascular Endurance

MILE INTERVAL RUN

Gary R. Fallon

Ithaca College, Princeton University, Washington and Lee University

Objective: To develop or maintain a desired level of cardiovascular endurance. Skills related to running are also incorporated.

Equipment Needed: Stopwatch

Description:

- Align four groups of drill participants at the four corners of the football field. Group members should be selected according to position and speed: (A) offensive and defensive linemen, (B) tight ends and defensive ends, (C) linebackers and running backs, and (D) wide receivers, quarterbacks, and defensive backs.
- A *position* coach is placed with each group.
- The drill coordinator is positioned in the middle of the field with a stopwatch and whistle.
- If staff size permits, other coaches are placed about the field to stress proper running form and motivate players.
- On the drill coordinator's whistle, all drill participants run completely around the field in a counterclockwise direction at a conditioning pace.
- This procedure is repeated four additional times with a rest interval of 25 seconds between each run.

Coaching Points:

- All running intervals start and stop on the drill coordinator's whistle.
- All drill participants begin their run behind a starting line and finish by running past a finish line.
- All runners should be encouraged to use fundamentally sound running form.
- For preseason conditioning, time intervals of 70 seconds should be set for the first week and 65 seconds for the second week. A standard of 60 seconds should be set for the regular season.
- The drill coordinator should call out the elapsed time at various intervals during each run.

Safety Considerations:

- A proper warm-up should precede the drill.
- The drill area should be clear of all foreign articles.
- The coach should closely monitor the fatigue level of all participants throughout the drill period.
- The training staff should be placed on special alert.
- The drill should not be conducted during extreme heat or high humidity conditions.

POST-PRACTICE CONDITIONING

Gene Murphy
University of North Dakota, California State University-Fullerton,
Fullerton Community College

Objective: To develop or maintain a desired level of cardiovascular endurance.

Equipment Needed: Stopwatch

Description:

- Divide the squad into three groups according to position and speed: (A) wide receivers, defensive backs, and running backs; (B) defensive ends, tight ends, linebackers, and quarterbacks; (C) offensive and defensive linemen. It is recommended that each group be given a special name such as Greyhounds, Aardvarks, and Spudbufts.
- Each group is positioned in a designated area behind a goal line.
- The drill coordinator is positioned at midfield with a stopwatch and a whistle.
- Other *position* coaches are aligned on the goal line and at designated turn-around points, and serve as motivators.
- On the drill coordinator's whistle, the first group runs from a starting stance on the goal line to the back of the end zone line on the opposite end of the field (110 yards). Each drill participant touches the back end zone line and returns to the original starting line (220 yards total).
- The drill continues until all groups have completed 10 repetitions of the 110/220 run.
- The following weekly running schedule and standards are recommended:
  - *Sunday*—10 x 110/220: Allow a time interval of one minute and 15 seconds between the start of the first run and the start of the second. The following front-end (110 yards) standards have been set: Group A—15 seconds; Group B—16 seconds; and Group C—17 seconds. The total elapsed time between the start and finish of the 10 runs is 12 minutes, 35 seconds.
  - *Monday*—10 x 75/150: Allow a time interval of 50 seconds between the start of the first run and the start of the second. No front-end time standards have been set for the 75/150. The total elapsed time between the start and finish of the 10 runs is eight minutes, 20 seconds.
  - *Tuesday*—10 x 55/110: Allow a time interval of 40 seconds between the start of the first run and the start of the second. No front-end time standards have been set for the 55/110. The total elapsed time between the start and finish of the 10 runs is six minutes, 40 seconds.

- *Wednesday*—10 x 40/80: Allow a time interval of 30 seconds between the start of the first run and the start of the second. No front-end time standards have been set for the 40/80. The total elapsed time between the start and finish of the 10 runs is five minutes.

- *Preseason*—Run 110/220s or 75/150s in the morning and 55/110s or 40/80s in the afternoon.

Coaching Points:

- All running intervals start and stop on the drill coordinator's whistle.
- All drill participants begin their run behind the goal line and run through and touch the designated turn-around points and then run through the finish line.
- All personnel should be encouraged to use fundamentally sound principles of running.
- The drill coordinator should call out the elapsed time at various intervals during each run.

Safety Considerations:

- A proper warm-up should precede the drill.
- The drill area should be clear of all foreign articles.
- The coach should closely monitor the fatigue level of all participants throughout the drill period.
- The training staff should be placed on special alert.
- The drill should not be conducted during extreme heat or high humidity conditions.

300-YARD SHUTTLE RUN*

> ## William "Mack" Brown
> Appalachian State University, Tulane University,
> University of North Carolina, University of Texas

Objective: To test for and develop or maintain a desired level of cardiovascular endurance. Incorporated are skills related to agility and quickness. The test can be administered on the summer reporting date and at the conclusion of the winter conditioning program. Time-interval standards for the shuttle run are correlated with the individual's 40-time (4.6-40–under 46.0 second shuttle run; 5.2-40–under 52.0 shuttle run, etc.).

Equipment Needed: Stopwatch and four cones

Description:

- Align two cones five-yards apart from the midpoint of a selected goal line. Two additional cones are placed in corresponding positions on the 50-yard line.
- All the drill participants are positioned adjacent to the start area on the goal line.
- One coach is placed near the goal line and one on the 50-yard line.
- On the goal line coach's command, the first drill participant takes a stance behind starting line and sprints to and touches the 50-yard line and returns to the goal line. Procedure is repeated until drill participant has covered 300 yards.
- The goal line coach monitors each drill participant's time and starts his watch on the runner's first movement.
- The drill continues until all the drill participants have run a sufficient number of 300-yard shuttle runs.

Coaching Points:

- Insist that all the drill participants begin each shuttle run from behind the goal line and run through and touch all designated turn-around points.
- Make sure that all the runners run past the finish line.
- All the runners should be encouraged to use fundamentally sound principles of running.

* Reprinted with permission from *101 Winning Football Drills: From the Legends of the Game* by Jerry Tolley

Safety Considerations:

- A proper warm-up should precede the drill.
- The drill area should be clear of all foreign articles.
- Coaches should monitor closely the fatigue level of all the drill participants throughout the drill period.
- The training staff should be placed on special alert.
- It is imperative that each drill participant be given a five-minute rest period after he has concluded his shuttle run.
- The drill should not be conducted during extreme heat or high humidity conditions.

Variation:

- Can have two or more drill participants run course at the same time.

SPEEDY SPRINTS

Chuck Mills
Utah State University, Wake Forest University, The Coast Guard Academy, Southern Oregon State College, Indiana University (PA), Pomona College, United State Merchant Marine Academy, Kansas City Chiefs

Objective: To develop or maintain a desired level of cardiovascular endurance.

Equipment Needed: Six large blocking dummies and three footballs

Description:

- Divide the squad into six groups according to position and speed (tight ends and quarterbacks; linebackers and defensive ends; defensive and offensive linemen; offensive backs and receivers; and defensive backs).

- Align three dummies 10 yards apart on a selected goal line. Place three additional dummies in corresponding positions on the 40-yard line.

- Position the three offensive groups on the goal line facing downfield. One group each is positioned to the right of each of the three dummies. All drill participants are aligned in pairs.

- The three defensive groups are positioned in a corresponding alignment on the 40 yard line facing the goal line. Again, one group each is positioned to the right of the three dummies.

- A coach is stationed in front of, and to the right of, each group.

- On the group coach's command (verbal for offensive personnel and simulated ball snap for defensive personnel), the first pair of drill participants drives from their stances and sprint the 40-yard distance.

- The procedure is continued until all paired drill participants have run the 40-yard course.

- The sprints are then repeated with all paired drill participants returning to their original starting positions.

- The drill continues until all drill participants have had a sufficient number of repetitions.

Coaching Points:

- Insist that all drill participants begin each sprint from behind the designated starting line and in the desired stance.

- Make sure all drill participants sprint past the designated finish line.

- All drill participants should be encouraged to use fundamentally sound principles of running.

Safety Considerations:

- A proper warm-up should precede the drill.
- The drill area should be clear of all foreign articles.
- The coach should closely monitor the fatigue level of all participants throughout the drill period.
- The training staff should be placed on special alert.
- The drill should not be conducted during extreme heat or high humidity conditions.

Variations:

- Can vary the sprinting distance between the dummies.
- Can have individual challenges between the paired sprinters.

TEAM-KICKOFF CONDITIONING*

Ronald "Ron" Randleman
William Penn College, Pittsburg State University, Sam Houston State University
National Coach of the Year: Pittsburg State 1981

Objective: To develop or maintain a desired level of cardiovascular endurance while teaching the basics of covering a kickoff.

Equipment Needed: 10 cones, kicking tee, and a football

Description:

- Place ten cones on a football field representing the pre-kickoff return alignment of a receiving kickoff team. Kickoff returners are aligned in their normal kickoff return position at the goal line.

- Position the number one kickoff-coverage team in its regular kickoff alignment. All other players with the exception of offensive linemen line up behind the first kickoff team.

- On the coach's whistle, the kicker executes the kickoff and the number one kickoff-coverage team sprints full speed downfield covering the kick.

- The first kick returner catches the football and returns it approximately 10 yards upfield in a designated direction and then comes to a stop.

- All the kickoff coverage personnel continue sprinting through their designated coverage lanes and then *squeeze* down on the kick returner. As the kickoff team approaches the kick returner, all the coverage personnel break down in the basic football position *buzzing* their feet.

- On the coach's command, the coverage team sprints to the near sideline and the kick returner sprints upfield for the touchdown.

- The kickoff coverage team now jogs back down the sideline and prepares for their next kickoff coverage. The kick returner does the same.

- The drill continues until all the drill participants have had a sufficient number of repetitions.

---

* Reprinted with permission from *101 Winning Football Drills: From the Legends of the Game* by Jerry Tolley

Coaching Points:

- Always check to see that all the kickoff coverage personnel are aligned correctly and are in their proper stances.
- Insist that all the kickoff coverage personnel sprint through their designated coverage lane before *squeezing* down on the kick returner.
- Make sure that all the kickoff coverage personnel break down in the basic football position and *buzz* their feet as they *squeeze* down on the kick returner.
- Instruct the kick returner to sprint toward the goal line after the kickoff coverage personnel sprint to the near sideline.

Safety Considerations:

- A proper warm-up should precede the drill.
- The drill area should be clear of all foreign articles. This includes both the sideline areas.
- The drill should not be conducted during extreme heat or high humidity conditions.
- The coach and training staff should monitor closely the fatigue level of all the drill participants throughout the drill period.

Variation:

- Can be used as a kickoff coverage drill.

12-MINUTE RUN*

Robert S. "Bob" Griffin
Idaho State University, University of Rhode Island, Berlin Adler-Germany, Syracuse University, College of the Holy Cross

Objective: To test for, develop, or maintain a desired level of cardiovascular endurance. This drill also can serve as the foundation for an off-season conditioning program.

Equipment Needed: Stopwatch

Description:

- Drill participants run for 12 minutes on a quarter-mile track or around a measured course. The following performance standards have been set:
  - *Linemen*. Run 6.5 laps on a quarter-mile track or 1.5 miles plus 220 yards in under 12 minutes.
  - *Backs and Receivers*. Run 7.5 laps on a quarter-mile track or one 1.75 miles plus 220 yards in under 12 minutes.
  - *Linebackers and Backs Over 200 pounds*. Run seven laps on a quarter-mile track or 1.75 miles in under 12 minutes.

Coaching Points:

- The drill can be self-administered or coach-administered.
- Individual time and lap count should be recorded at the conclusion of each 12-minute run.
- All drill participants should be encouraged to use fundamentally sound principles of running.
- The drill coordinator should call out the elapsed time as drill participants pass starting or check points.

* The author of the 12-minute run drill wishes to acknowledge Dr. Kenneth H. Cooper for the time and distance standards used.

Safety Considerations:

- A proper warm-up should precede the drill.
- The coach should closely monitor the fatigue level of all participants throughout the drill period.
- The training staff should be placed on special alert.
- The drill area should be clear of all foreign articles.
- The drill should not be conducted during extreme heat or high humidity conditions.

SHUTTLE RUN*

Bill Snyder
Kansas State University
National Coach of the Year: 1994 and 1998

Objective: To test for a desired level of cardiovascular endurance. Incorporated are skills related to running and changing directions.

Equipment Needed: Cones, stopwatches, notepads, and pencils

Description:

- Lay out a shuttle-running lane by placing two cones five yards apart on a selected line of scrimmage, and two additional cones five yards apart and 60 yards downfield. More shuttle lanes can be formed as necessary. (Eight shuttle lanes are recommended.)
- All the drill participants are positioned behind the start of the shuttle-running lanes.
- Coaches are positioned at each of the starting positions and serve as starters. Two additional coaches with stopwatches and a third coach who serves as a recorder are positioned at the finish line.
- On the starting coach's command, the first drill participant in each shuttle lane drives out of his stance and sprints from one end of the shuttle run to the other until 300 yards have been covered. (5x60 yards=300 yards)
- After completing the first shuttle run, each drill participant walks back to the starting line and is allowed a one-minute rest period before performing a second and final shuttle run.
- It is recommended that the average time of the two shuttle runs be equal to or below the drill participant's 40-yard sprint time multiplied by 10. (Example: If a player runs a 4.5 40-yard sprint, the average time of his two shuttle runs should be 45 seconds, because 4.5x10=45.)

Coaching Points:

- Insist that all the drill participants begin each shuttle run behind the designated starting point and in a designated stance.
- All the drill participants should be encouraged to use fundamentally sound principles of running.

---

* Reprinted with permission from *101 Winning Football Drills: From the Legends of the Game* by Jerry Tolley

- The emphasis should be placed on getting a good start.
- Instruct all the drill participants to touch, but not cross over, each ending line. They should not slow down in the turns, but enter each turn low making a half turn while touching the end line with the lead foot and then accelerating while completing the turn around.
- Instruct the drill participants that while both shuttle runs should be at near full speed, the first run should be at a pace two to four seconds faster than the required average time of the two shuttle runs. (Example: if a player runs a 4.5 40-yard sprint, his first shuttle run should be 45 seconds minus two to four seconds. His second shuttle run can be two to four seconds slower than the first run.)

Safety Considerations:

- A proper warm-up should precede the drill.
- The drill area should be clear of all foreign articles.
- The drill should not be conducted during extreme heat or high humidity conditions.
- The training staff should be placed on full alert.
- The coach and training staff should monitor closely the fatigue level of all the drill participants throughout the drill.
- A complete physical examination should precede all preseason cardiovascular-conditioning testing.

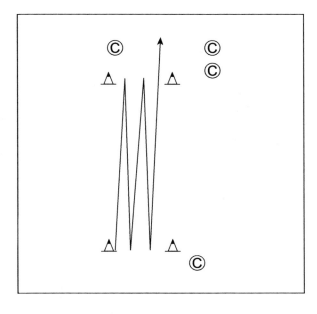

Appendices

Appendix A

Sports Medicine Guidelines*

Dr. Fred Mueller
University of North Carolina-Chapel Hill

Dr. Fred Mueller is Professor and Chairman of the Department of Exercise and Sport Science at The University of North Carolina at Chapel Hill. He currently serves as Director of the National Center for Catastrophic Sports Injury Research at UNC and is Chairman of the American Football Coaches Association Committee on Football Injuries. He is also a member of the American College of Sports Medicine. The following are his recommendations to help reduce football injuries and make the game safer for the participants.

Medical Exam

Mandatory medical examinations and medical history should be taken before allowing an athlete to participate in football. The National Collegiate Athletic Association recommends a thorough medical examination when the athlete first enters the college athletic program and an annual health-history update with use of referral exams when warranted. If the physician or coach has any questions about the athletes' readiness to participate, the athlete should not be allowed to play. High school coaches should follow the recommendations set by their state high school athletic association.

Health Insurance

Each student athlete should be covered by individual, parental, or institutional medical insurance to defray the costs of significant injury or illness. At the high school level, the schools should provide information about association-provided medical insurance.

Preseason Conditioning

All personnel concerned with training football athletes should emphasize proper, gradual, and complete physical conditioning. Special emphasis should be placed on working in hot and humid weather conditions. Recommendations are as follows:

- Athletes must have a physical examination with a history of previous heat illness and type of training activities before organized practice begins.

- Acclimate athletes to heat gradually by providing graduated practice sessions for the first 7 to 10 days and other abnormally hot or humid days.
- Know both the temperature and humidity since it is more difficult for the body to cool itself in high humidity. The use of a sling psychrometer is recommended to measure the relative humidity and anytime the wet-bulb temperature is over 78 degrees practice should be altered.
- Adjust activity levels and provide frequent rest periods. Rest in cool, shaded areas with some air movement and remove helmets and loosen or remove jerseys. Rest periods of 15 to 30 minutes should be provided during workouts of one hour.
- Provide adequate cold water replacement during practice. *Water should always be available and in unlimited quantities to the athletes—give water regularly.*
- Salt should be replaced daily and a liberal salting of the athletes' food will accomplish this purpose. Coaches should not give salt tablets to athletes. Attention must be given to water replacement.
- Athletes should weigh each day before and after practice. Weight charts should be checked each day in order to treat athletes who lose excessive weight.
- Clothing is important and a player should avoid using long sleeves and any excess clothing. Never use rubberized clothing or sweat suits.
- Some athletes are more susceptible to heat injury than others. These individuals are not accustomed to working out in the heat, may be overweight, or may be the eager athlete who constantly competes at his capacity. Athletes with previous heat problems should be watched closely.
- It is important to observe for signs of heat illness. Some trouble signs are nausea, incoherence, fatigue, weakness, vomiting, weak rapid pulse, flushed appearance, visual disturbance, and unsteadiness. If heat illness is suspected, seek a physician's immediate service.

Facilities

It is the responsibility of the school administration to provide excellent facilities for the athletic program. The coach must monitor these facilities and keep them in the best condition.

Emergency Procedures

Each institution should strive to have a certified athletic trainer who is also a member of the school faculty. A team physician should be available for all games and readily available in other situations. There should also be a written emergency-procedure plan in place for catastrophic or serious injuries. All of the trainers and coaches should be familiar with the emergency plan.

Head and Neck Injuries

Coaches should continue to teach and emphasize the proper fundamentals of blocking and tackling to help reduce head and neck injuries. When a player has experienced or shown signs of head trauma (loss of consciousness, visual disturbances, headache, inability to walk correctly, obvious disorientation, memory loss), he should receive immediate medical attention and should not be allowed to return to practice or a game without permission from the proper medical authorities.

Records

Adequate and complete records of each injury should be kept and analyzed to determine injury patterns and to make recommendations for prevention.

Final Recommendations

- Strict enforcement of the rules of the game by both coaches and officials will help reduce injuries.
- You must keep the head out of blocking and tackling. *Keep the head out of football.*
- There should be a renewed emphasis on employing well-trained athletic personnel, providing excellent facilities, and securing the safest and best equipment available.

* Reprinted with permission from *101 Winning Football Drills: From the Legends of the Game* by Jerry Tolley

Appendix B

Medical and Legal Considerations*

Dr. Herb Appenzeller
Guilford College

Dr. Herb Appenzeller is a former athletics director at Guilford College and Professor of Sports Management Emeritus. He is also a former football coach. He has authored and edited 16 books in the area of sport law, risk management, and sport management. He is the co-editor of *From The Gym To The Jury*, a sport-law newsletter. He is a member of four sports Halls of Fame. At the present, he is Executive-in-Residence in graduate Sport Administration at Appalachian State University.

No one wants an athlete to be injured. In sports activities, however, there is always the possibility of injury no matter how careful you are in observing proper procedures. And no one wants to be involved in a lawsuit. Today we have an unprecedented number of sports-related litigation that concerns everyone associated with sports.

The fact that injury occurs does not necessarily mean that the coach is negligent or liable for damages. No sure criteria exist for determining what is negligent action since each case stands individually on its own merit. The following recommendations can help prevent situations that may lead to injuries or litigation:

- Require a thorough physical examination before the athlete engages in the sport.

- Assign someone to make certain all equipment fits properly.

- Assign someone to inspect equipment for defects and the facilities for hazards. Keep an accurate record of each inspection.

- Obtain medical insurance coverage for the athlete and liability insurance for the coaches and other staff members.

- Adopt a medical plan for emergency treatment for all athletes involved in physical contact or strenuous exercise.

- Assign drills within the athlete's range of ability and commensurate with his size, skill, and physical condition.

- Prepare the athlete gradually for all physical drills and progress from simple to complex tasks in strenuous and dangerous drills.

- Warn the athlete of all possible dangers inherent in the drills in which he is involved.
- Follow the activities as designed. If the coach deviates from the prescribed drills, the decision to do so should be based on sound reasoning. Extra precautions for safety should be taken.
- Adopt a policy regarding injuries. Do not attempt to be a medical specialist in judging the physical condition of an athlete under your care.
- Require a physician's medical permission before permitting seriously injured or ill athletes to return to normal practice.
- Avoid moving the injured athlete until it is safe to do so. Whenever the athlete is moved, make certain he is taken away from potentially dangerous playing areas.
- Conduct periodic medical/legal in-service training programs for all personnel.

Risk management has become a vital part of the overall athletics program and football coaches should develop risk management strategies as they relate to their use of drills such as:

- Avoid terminology such as *suicide drills, death run, and hamburger drill*. These terms could come back to haunt you in court.
- In the event of an injury, always follow up with a call or visit to check on the athlete's condition. However, never, never admit fault or assign blame.
- Isolate and keep under lock and key equipment involved in a serious injury (helmet, protective pads, etc.).
- Be aware that you can be sued, but don't panic. Be prepared and coach with confidence.

* Reprinted with permission from *101 Winning Football Drills: From the Legends of the Game* by Jerry Tolley

Appendix C

Summer Two-A-Day Practice Guidelines*

The American Football Coaches Association and the National Athletic Trainers' Association have launched a new educational initiative, HEAT (Helping Educate Athletes in Training). The program is designed to help coaches better prepare their athletes for the grueling conditions of two-a-day practices.

These two-a-day workouts allow for accelerated physical conditioning, increased strength training, and skill development, and can even help develop bonds between teammates. But because these workouts usually occur in hot summer months, heat-related stress becomes a serious concern. Studies have shown that football players can lose dangerously high levels of fluid in 24 hours during two-a-day workouts. Additionally, athletes who are not properly acclimatized to the heat are highly susceptible to injury.

Tips for Safer Two-A-Days

Injury rates increase during two-a-day workouts whether athletes are in peak physical condition or not. In fact, many athletes don't even make their starting lineup because of injuries incurred during preseason training. The following tips can help ensure that athletes stay at their best and prevent heat-related injuries during two-a-days.

Encourage Athletes to Begin Conditioning Before Two-A-Days

Encourage athletes to begin conditioning in the heat two weeks before official practice begins. This allows their bodies to cool more efficiently by increasing sweat production sooner than when they are not acclimated to the heat.

Avoid Workouts During Unusually Hot Temperature

Practice sessions during unusually hot and humid conditions should be limited to very moderate workouts, postponed until cooler time of the day, or brought inside to avoid the heat.

Make Fluids Part of the Playbook

Before, during, and after competition, be sure to consume adequate amounts of fluid. Athletes can make sure they are properly hydrated by checking their urine color: lighter

*Printed with the permission of the **AFCA** and the **NATA** from their summer **HEAT** publication.*

urine color indicates athletes are better hydrated. The longer the workout session, the more frequently fluids need to be replaced. Research shows that a sports drink containing a six percent carbohydrate solution, like Gatorade, can be absorbed as rapidly as water. But unlike water, a sports drink can provide energy, delay fatigue, and improve performance.

Use the Shade

Before practice, warm up in the shade and be sure to rest in the shade during breaks. Even during rest, exposure to heat can raise the body temperature, increase fluid loss, and decrease the blood available to the muscles during workouts.

Recommend Wearing Loose Fitting Clothing

Cotton blend, loose fitting clothing can help promote heat loss. The rule: the less clothing, the better.

Be Prepared for an Emergency

Always have a cell phone on hand and be familiar with emergency numbers. Also keep ice and ice towels on hand in case of heat-related emergencies.

Fluids Guidelines for Two-A-Days

Proper hydration is the best safeguard against heat illness. Remember to have athletes drink before, during, and after training and competition. The following fluid consumption guidelines can help safeguard athletes against heat-related illness.

Before Exercise

- Two to three hours before exercise drink at least 17 to 20 oz. of water or sports drink.
- Ten to twenty minutes before exercise drink another 7 to 10 oz. of water or sports drink.

What to Drink During Exercise

- Drink early—even minimal dehydration compromises performance. In general, every 10 to 20 minutes drink at least 7 to 10 oz. of water or sports drink. To maintain hydration remember to drink beyond thirst. Optimally, drink fluids based on amount of heat and urine loss.
- Athletes benefit in many situations from drinking a sports drink containing carbohydrate.
- If exercise lasts more than 45 to 50 minutes or is intense, a sports drink should be provided during the session.

- The carbohydrate concentration in the ideal fluid replacement solution should be in the range of six to eight percent (14 g/8 oz.).

- During events when a high rate of fluid intake is necessary to sustain hydration, sport drink with less than seven percent carbohydrate should be used to optimize delivery.

- Fluid with salt (sodium chloride) are beneficial to increasing thirst and voluntary fluid intake as well as offsetting the amount in lost sweat.

- Cool beverages at temperatures of 50 to 59 degrees Fahrenheit are recommended.

What Not to Drink During Exercise

- Fruit juices, carbohydrate gels, sodas, and those sports drinks that have carbohydrate levels greater than 8% area not recommended as the sole beverage.

- Beverages containing caffeine, alcohol, and carbonation are discouraged during exercises because they can dehydrate the body by stimulating excess urine production, or decrease voluntary fluid intake.

After Exercises

Immediately after training or competition is the key time to replace fluids. Weigh athletes before and after exercise. Research indicates that for every pound of weight lost, athletes should drink at least 20 oz. of fluid to optimize rehydration. Sports beverages are an excellent choice.

About the Author

Jerry R. Tolley is the former head football coach at Elon University. Under his leadership, Elon earned a 49-11-2 record, claiming consecutive national titles in 1980 and 1981. His 1977 and 1978 squads were nationally ranked number six and number two, respectively. During his five-year head-coaching career, his teams garnered an 8-1 record in playoff bowl competition and won an impressive 80.6 % of all games played.

During his career, Tolley received numerous coaching honors, including conference, district, state, area, and national coach of the year awards. In January 2003, he received the lifetime membership award from the American Football Coaches Association and in June of 2003 received the Johnny Vaught Lifetime Achievement Award from the All-American Football Foundation. He has also received the National Football Foundation Hall of Fame Dwight D. Eisenhower award as well as the State of North Carolina Order of the Long Leaf Pine Award and the Laurel Wreath Award, the highest award given by the State of North Carolina in the area of sports and athletics. Tolley is also a member of Omicron Delta Kappa, the national leadership fraternity.

Tolley is listed in numerous Who's Who volumes, including Marquis Who's Who in America, in the World, in the South and Southwest, in Business and Finance, and in Science and Engineering. He is also listed in *Who's Who among Community Leaders in America*, *Who's Who in Government Services*, and *Who's Who among World Intellectuals*.

Dr. Tolley's first book, *The American Football Coaches Guide Book To Championship Football Drills*, was published in 1984. His second book, *101 Winning Football Drills: From the Legends of the Game*, was released in 2003. He has also written numerous football-related articles for *Coach and Athlete*, *The Athletic Journal*, *The Coaching Clinic*, and the *Journal of Health Physical Education, Recreation, and Dance*. His doctoral dissertation was "The History of Intercollegiate Athletics for Men at Elon College."

Since his retirement from coaching, Dr. Tolley continues to serve Elon University as the director of annual giving. He is also involved in a number of community activities, having served two terms as mayor of the town of Elon, as well as on many local boards, including The Alamance Foundation, The Thomas E. Powell Jr. Biology Foundation, The Community Foundation of Greater Greensboro, The Alamance Education Alliance, and BEACTIVE North Carolina.